The Teaching of Ethics XI

The Teaching of Social Work Ethics

Frederic G. Reamer
Marcia Abramson

INSTITUTE OF
SOCIETY, ETHICS AND
THE LIFE
SCIENCES THE
HASTINGS
CENTER

The Hastings Center
Institute of Society, Ethics and the Life Sciences
360 Broadway
Hastings-on-Hudson, New York 10706

Library of Congress Cataloging in Publication Data

Reamer, Frederic G., 1953-
  The teaching of social work ethics.

  (The Teaching of ethics ; 11)
  Bibliography: p.
  1. Social service—Moral and ethical aspects—Study
and teaching. I. Abramson, Marcia, joint author. II. Title.
III. Series.
HV11.R36   174'.9362'07   81-86582
ISBN 0-916558-15-0   AACR2

Printed in the United States of America

Contents

FOREWORD

A concern for the ethical instruction and formation of students has always been a part of American higher education. Yet that concern has by no means been uniform or free of controversy. The centrality of moral philosophy in the undergraduate curriculum during the mid-nineteenth century gave way later during that century to the first signs of increasing specialization of the disciplines. By the middle of the twentieth century, instruction in ethics had, by and large, become confined almost exclusively to departments of philosophy and religion. Efforts to introduce ethics teaching in the professional schools and elsewhere in the university often met with indifference or outright hostility.

The past decade has seen a remarkable resurgence of interest in the teaching of ethics at both the undergraduate and professional school levels. Beginning in 1977, The Hastings Center, with the support of the Rockefeller Brothers Fund and the Carnegie Corporation of New York, undertook a systematic study of the teaching of ethics in American higher education. Our concern focused on the extent and quality of that teaching, and on the main possibilities and problems posed by widespread efforts to find a more central and significant role for ethics in the curriculum.

As part of that project, a number of papers, studies, and monographs were commissioned. Moreover, in an attempt to gain some degree of consensus, the authors of those studies worked together as a group for a period of two years. The study presented here represents one outcome of the project. We hope and believe it will be helpful for those concerned to advance and deepen the teaching of ethics in higher education.

Daniel Callahan   Sissela Bok
Project Co-Directors
The Hastings Center
Project on the Teaching of Ethics

About the Authors

Frederic G. Reamer

Frederic Reamer is an assistant professor at the School of Social Work, University of Missouri–Columbia. His principal areas of interest include the study of criminal and juvenile justice, child welfare, and social work ethics. He completed his undergraduate work at the University of Maryland–College Park and received his A.M. and Ph.D. from the University of Chicago. Professor Reamer has served on the faculty of the University of Chicago, School of Social Service Administration, and has been actively involved in efforts of the federal Office of Juvenile Justice and Delinquency Prevention to plan and evaluate social service programs for juvenile offenders. He has written on the subjects of juvenile justice, child welfare, and social work ethics, and is the author of the forthcoming *Ethical Dilemmas in Social Service* (Columbia University Press).

Marcia Abramson

Marcia Abramson is an assistant professor at Columbia University School of Social Work where she teaches social work practice. She is a clinical investigator on the Research Project in Issues of Values and Ethics in Health Care at the Columbia Presbyterian Medical Center. She received her B.A. from Bennington College, her Master's in Social Service from Syracuse University School of Social Work, and a Ph.D. from the University of Iowa. Her scholarly interests lie in ethical dilemmas in health care delivery, particularly interdisciplinary collaboration and long-term care.

Preface

The nature of social work has changed dramatically since its emergence as a profession in the nineteenth century. During the early years of the profession's history, around the turn of the century, social workers were primarily concerned with the poor and their problems. Organizing relief and responding to the "curse of pauperism"[1] were principal missions of the profession. The full armamentaria of the charity organization societies, "friendly visitors," unions, and other self-help groups were directed toward what Alexander Johnson has referred to as "the dreary prospect of human misery" which characterized this era.[2] The aims of social work today are much broader. Social workers are no longer wholly preoccupied with the plight of the poor. In increasing numbers, social workers are serving more affluent populations and individuals whose problems relate to being handicapped, delinquent, old, mentally disturbed, displaced, deserted, and unhappy. The methods of social work have also changed over time. Practitioners in contemporary schools of social work can now be trained in methods that include group work, behavioral techniques, community organization, public administration, and research, in addition to learning traditional casework skills. Further, the interventions of social workers are no longer confined to local boundaries; their professional activities and vision now include the development of programs and policies for entire regions, states, and the nation as a whole.

Despite the substantial changes in the complexion of the profession of social work, there has been, throughout its history, a concern about morality and ethics. As with the profession itself, however, the nature of this concern has changed over time. During the earliest years of the profession, around the time of the charity organization societies, the principal concern was with the morality of the pauper, in particular, his moral failings. The mission of social workers was to help the poor and destitute discover the errors of their wayward lives and to exhort them to embrace the virtues of hard work, temperance, and providence. Concern about the moral rectitude of the poor waned considerably—though not entirely—during the rise of the settlement house movement in the early twentieth century, when the attention of many social workers shifted from attempts to reform the moral backbone of the poor to attempts to reform the social conditions that appeared to induce poverty and allow it to breed.

Concern about the morality of the client continued to recede somewhat during the next several decades of the profession's life, as practitioners engaged in earnest attempts to establish and polish its techniques, training programs, and schools of thought—the "art and science" of social work. Eventually, morality took a back seat to what evolved into a central debate about the future of the profession, that is, "whether to continue along the lines of the psycho-social casework expounded by Mary Richmond and being practiced or whether to embrace the psychotherapy which some psychiatric social workers were beginning to view with favor,"[3] and whether to incorporate the study of social welfare policy and social development into the profession.

By 1950, however, concerns about moral aspects of social work began emerging with greater frequency, though in very different clothes. Unlike the pervasive concern during the nineteenth century with the morality of the client (pauper), the concern that emerged during the mid-years of the twentieth century began to lean toward the morality and ethics of the profession of social work and of its practitioners. Attention focused on developing ethical guidelines in order to promote proper conduct among social workers. In 1947, after several years of debate and discusson, the Delegate Conference of the American Association of Social Workers adopted a code of ethics. Literature concerning social work ethics began to appear in the profession's journals with greater frequency. In 1959 Muriel Pumphrey published her landmark work on the teaching of values and ethics in social work.[4] The era around the fifties thus represents an important period for the subject of social work ethics.[5] It was during these years that serious interest in the subject began to unfold.

The profession has come a long way in the intervening years. We have witnessed a considerable expansion of professional interests and methods. We have gone beyond a mere flirtation with science and the scientific method, having embraced empiricism and methods of research as an integral part of the training of contemporary social workers. In the midst of these developments, however, many of us have come to recognize—or have had reaffirmed—the fact that there are limits to the answers science and empirical methods can provide, as well as limits to the answers that discourse about social work techniques (the art of practice) can provide. We have come to realize that there are aspects of social work practice that are ethical in nature, either because they raise serious questions about the values that guide our professional activities and decisions, or because we frequently face difficult dilemmas that require us to make disquieting choices based on our beliefs about what is right and wrong, or good and bad, in a moral sense. We know now that science cannot tell us when it may be appropriate to reveal confidential information shared by a client, or whether the whistle ought to be blown on a colleague who has engaged in some impropriety. We know now that theories of social casework and of other forms of intervention cannot, by themselves, tell us whether it is permissible to lie to a fragile client who has inquired about her progress, or to willfully violate an agency policy or a law we consider to be unjust. These are, after all, dilemmas that raise important questions of ethics.

We believe it is important for social workers to be sensitive to the variety of ethical issues and dilemmas that can and does arise in practice. More specifically, we believe that an introduction to the subject of social work ethics should be included in the training and continuing education of social workers. In this monograph we address a range of issues related to the subject of social work ethics. We have organized our discussion into three major sections. In the first we provide a brief overview of the current status of social work ethics and the teaching of it. In Section II we review a number of substantive issues related to social work ethics that we believe deserve attention in attempts to introduce students and practitioners to this subject. In Section III we discuss in some detail various ways in which the teaching of social work ethics can be approached; in this section we address such topics as educational goals, pedagogical techniques, placement in the curriculum, and instructor qualifications and training. Our hope and intention is that this discussion will assist those individuals who are interested in introducing and promoting the teaching of social work ethics.

We would like to acknowledge the helpful assistance of Judith Mishne in the preparation of this monograph.

I. The Place of Ethics in Social Work

Within the past fifteen years there has been a dramatic increase in the amount of attention paid to the general subject of professional ethics. This fact is demonstrated by three developments within this period. First, a number of organizations have been created whose primary purpose has been to foster the study of applied and professional ethics. These organizations include The Hastings Center (Institute of Society, Ethics and the Life Sciences), the Kennedy Institute of Ethics at Georgetown University, the Center for Philosophy and Public Policy at the University of Maryland, the Westminster Institute for Ethics and Human Values, the Center for the Study of Values at the University of Delaware, and the Center for the Study of Ethics in the Professions at the Illinois Institute of Technology. Although much of the attention of these organizations has been devoted to the fields of medical ethics and bioethics, as a group they have expanded their boundaries in recent years to include the study of ethical issues in fields such as law, journalism, nursing, business, engineering, public policy, social science, and social work. These organizations have done much to stimulate and focus attention upon ethical problems in the professions through their writings, workshops, and other ancillary activities.

A second indicator of the enormous growth of interest in applied and professional ethics is the published (and unpublished) literature that has emerged within the past ten to fifteen years. Although certainly there are essays to be found on the subject of professional ethics written before 1970, the volume of literature produced prior to this date pales against the dramatic outpouring of literature we have experienced since then. Again, the bulk of this relatively recent literature concerns medical ethics and bioethics, but it is clear that the production in other fields has accelerated as well, though at a slower pace.

Finally, recent surveys indicate that within the past fifteen years (and especially within the past decade), the amount of time (and space) devoted to the subject of applied and professional ethics in colleges and universities has grown at a rapid rate. This is reflected in the increased number of courses being taught on the subject and in the amount of time devoted to ethical issues in nonethics courses. In 1980, The Hastings Center published the results of a survey of courses being taught on the subject of ethics in colleges, universities, and professional schools.[6] The survey included a review of course listings for 1977 and 1978 in school catalogues for a sample that covered approximately one-fourth of all institutions of higher education in the United States (623 out of 2,270 institutions), A total of 2,757 of the surveyed courses were concerned with ethics. Nearly one-fifth of the courses listed in the catalogues were placed in the category of professional ethics. Two-fifths of the courses included ethics as a major theme, and the remainder listed ethics as a subtheme. The number of applied ethics courses was about the same as the number of courses devoted to theoretical ethics, although the ratio of applied courses to theoretical courses varied considerably from school to school. Most of the applied ethics courses were in the areas of medicine, business, and law. Approximately one-fourth of the surveyed courses were taught by a department of philosophy, and one-seventh of the courses were taught by a religious studies department; the rest were taught in various departments and schools throughout the colleges and universities.[7]

The results of The Hastings Center survey demonstrated several significant changes in the amount and type of attention devoted to the subject of ethics since the previous decade:

A comparative sampling of ethics offerings in philosophy departments from the period 1950–65 revealed very few courses in "applied ethics." Moreover, most of the textbooks and readers used during that period focused very broadly on theoretical questions of ethics. The most important change within the past decade has been an increasing emphasis in textbooks and readers on very concrete issues in ethics: abortion, truth-telling, confidentiality, justice, war and peace, sexual ethics, and the like. No less noteworthy has been the rapid proliferation of courses outside traditional philosophy and religious studies departments, almost all of them with an applied focus. Thus significant content changes are underway in those departments that have traditionally taught ethics, and the introduction of courses in ethics in other departments and divisions of the university is itself a notable phenomenon.[8]

A. The Growth of Professional Ethics

What explains this relatively recent surge of interest in applied and professional ethics? Certainly no one factor alone accounts for the growth of activity in this area. As with the emergence of many intellectual subjects, there are several determinants. The relatively recent growth of interest in professional ethics has arisen in part, it appears, because of the invention of new technologies which have forced practitioners to make ethical decisions which were not called for in the past. This is most apparent in the medical field, where pharmaceutical and technical advances (for example, the invention of life-sustaining equipment) have brought with them the onus of difficult decisions about when they should be used, for whom they should be used, and under what conditions they can be justifiably withdrawn.

A second factor which apparently has heightened the curiosity of professionals about ethical issues is related to the growing awareness that many of the resources that were at one time plentiful are now limited (for example, support for public programs, health care, legal aid) and that decisions need to be made about the criteria that should be used to distribute them. Questions concerning the need for government regulations designed to guide the distribution of limited resources have added to the complexity of this challenge.

A third factor stems from the swelling skepticism among the public about the methods and morality of public officials and professionals. It is common knowledge now that the sins of Watergate, ABSCAM, the awarding of a Pulitzer Prize for a bogus newspaper series, and sundry other national and local scandals have done much to shake public confidence in professionals. Such events have led professionals as well to scurry to clean their own houses, lest some guest, invited or otherwise, check for incriminating dust with white gloves. Concern among the public is also enhanced by the common and contagious anxiety about the erosion of traditional values and mores (especially following the social upheaval of the 1960s), the instability in the lives of many families, and the insidious growth of crime and delinquency which strikes a collective nerve.

Two other factors, of a somewhat different order, also seem to account for the growth of interest in professional ethics. One has to do with a greater appreciation by professionals in recent years that there are limits to the answers that science and research can provide, and an accompanying realization that questions that science by itself is unable to answer frequently reduce to ethical questions. This point of view contrasts sharply with logical positivism and the near-worship of science and the scientific method which characterized the mid-years of the twentieth century, when high hopes were held that we would be able to use classic experimental designs, complex operational indicators, and multivariate data analysis techniques to order our world, understand it, and reveal the nature of the causal relationships it contained. As Frederick Suppe has observed: "Consider the classical philosophical theses that an absolute causal account can be given of phenomena, that ultimate laws of a deterministic sort can be gleaned from natural phenomena, and that some rock-bed of perceptual certainty is necessary to gain a firm knowledge of the world. All three of these theses are false and hopelessly out of date in terms of the kinds of theories now coming to dominate science."[9]

The second factor is related to what might be described as a function of the maturation of professions. The early years and decades of professions generally seem to be devoted to developing techniques, schools of thought, and training programs. The very *raison d'etre* of a profession would seem to depend upon the visibility and stability of such intellectual apparatus. Though exceptions can no doubt be found, it is not surprising that the professions, as a group, have only relatively recently begun searching out and addressing normative questions and ethical issues. Given the history of the world, professions are relatively recent inventions, the early chapters of which appear to have been devoted primarily to the development of their technical, rather than normative, foundations.

B. The Status of Social Work Ethics

These factors no doubt explain, at least in part, the emergence of interest in social work ethics since the 1950s and, especially, within the past decade. For example, the decisions that hospital social workers face today have grown out of technological advances in medicine that require very difficult professional judgments about truth-telling, the right to self-determination, and the distribution of scarce resources. Social workers, along with their colleagues in other fields, have also borne the brunt of public skepticism about the methods and morals of professionals. Further, social work is young, barely a century old; as with many of the professions, during its earliest years social work practitioners were preoccupied with developing and refining the technical tools and methods of the trade in an attempt to solidify its foundation (in its own eyes as well as in the eyes of others), rather than concentrating on normative issues that could at times broach threatening questions about the mission of social work.

But there are important differences between the ways in which interest in social work ethics has developed and the ways in which interest in ethical issues has developed in other professions. When compared with the fields of medicine and law, for example, social work is somewhat less developed in the area of professional ethics. This is especially evident in two respects. First, while there is ample evidence that there has been a growing stream of literature on ethical issues in the other professions, one is hard pressed to assemble more than a large handful of writings devoted specifically to the subject of social work ethics. There are numerous writings in journals and introductory texts on the general subject of values, but there are literally only several writings which address the subject of social work ethics in a disciplined, systematic fashion, with some regard to the relationship between the tradition of thought and ideas in moral philosophy and contemporary ethical problems of the profession. What literature is available in social work tends to concentrate on fairly superficial discussions of traditional (though admittedly important) values such as respecting client dignity, promoting self-determination and equity, maintaining confidentiality, and so on. The number of articles that discuss questions regarding the justification of social work values, and problems that practitioners encounter attempting to resolve conflicts among them, is relatively small. The dearth of literature on social work ethics contrasts dramatically with the wealth of literature on ethical issues in the fields of medicine and law, and the steadily increasing literatures in the fields of business, nursing, journalism, engineering, and the social sciences.[10]

Second, the perceptible increase in the number of courses, portions of courses, and other educational offerings on the subject of ethics, which has characterized other professions, has not, as a rule, been characteristic of social work. Our efforts to identify discrete courses on the subject of social work ethics being taught in graduate programs, although not entirely systematic and exhaustive, turned up a mere handful. We assume that there are many instructors who address, at least to some extent, the subject of social work ethics within the context of other courses in the curriculum (for example, in methods courses, policy courses, and courses on research), but we have no evidence that the curricula of social work programs generally include instruction on this subject in any systematic or deliberate fashion.

That the amount of attention devoted to ethical issues in social work, as displayed in its literature and training programs, has been lacking, especially when compared with other professions, strikes us as a very curious phenomenon. Of the many professions that now dot the contemporary landscape, social work is among the most normative. As we noted earlier, our professional history began with strong convictions about the morality of paupers and about the need to strengthen and bolster their character. And the decisions made by present-day social workers are rife with ethical judgments about such matters as the need to intervene in individuals' lives, the extent to which social workers should actively shape the direction of clients' lives, clients' right to self-determination, social justice, the role of government and the free market in welfare matters, the allocation of scarce resources, social reform, and so on. It is both perplexing and disconcerting that members of the social work profession have not paid more explicit attention to ethical issues.

C. Apparent Determinants

What might account for this state of affairs? It is, of course, not possible to isolate a single factor that would explain why social workers have been slower to develop a focused and deliberate interest in ethics than have members of other professions. Undoubtedly, several factors account for this rather glaring discrepancy. We would like to speculate about four that we believe may help to explain the relative lack of attention to social work ethics.

First, it is interesting to note that in many other professions, the amount of attention paid to ethical issues has apparently increased as skepticism about the capacity of science to resolve professional conundrums has increased. We noted earlier that in many professions, the expectations of scholars and practitioners about the likely contributions of empirical research and science have become more modest, and they have, as a result, shifted part of their attention to questions of ethics. Many professionals now understand the weaknesses and limitations of standard research methods (for example, with respect to enduring problems of validity, reliability, specifying adequate operational indicators, and so on) and the possibility that even well-designed studies often do not produce results whose normative implications are clear. What Hume long ago labeled the "is-ought" problem has turned out to be a persistent gadfly for many researchers and practitioners. However, what has been true of other professions has apparently not been true for social work. As a group we have begun to use the language and methods of research more than ever before. Training programs have added research requirements where none previously appeared, or have substantially upgraded them. Faculty, more than ever before, are judged by the quantity and quality of their empirical research. New emphases on "single-case designs," "the integration of research and practice," and the "practitioner-researcher," have emerged. Whether or not this movement is desirable is a separate question. What is relevant here is that social work has embraced an intellectual mission which, to some extent, has lost favor in many other fields.[11] A practical consequence has been, we believe, that the heightened attention to science and research has diverted attention from normative or ethical questions. It is possible that in this respect social work is in a developmental phase that simply lags behind certain other professions.

A second factor that may help to explain the modest degree of interest in social work ethics over the years is related to practitioners' views of themselves and their profession. Social workers are generally considered, and generally consider themselves, to be a group of altruistic professionals whose intentions are patently benevolent. Whether or not this is a deserved or accurate characterization is an open question—some would argue, for example, that social workers have frequently served as agents of the middle and upper classes and have, with somewhat self-interested motives, functioned as preservers of the status quo and of a conservative social order. Whatever motives have been attributed to social workers, throughout our history we have generally regarded ourselves as "doers of good." It might be argued that as a result social workers have not felt the same urgency that practitioners in other fields have felt about the need to raise ethical issues concerning professional morality. Social workers who have viewed themselves as noble practitioners with only the most benevolent of intentions have perhaps not thought it necessary to scratch beneath the surface of the apparently virtuous veneer of the profession in order to examine the morality of the interior, less public areas of social work. This is a thesis that, though conjectural, appears to be supported by historical accounts of the development of social work and of practitioners' views of their purposes and mission.[12]

A third factor is related more closely to the view practitioners have of the extent to which social work has achieved the status of a full-fledged profession. While there may be little doubt among contemporary practitioners about social work's status as a profession, it is clear that throughout its history doubt has lingered—more evidently during some periods than others—about whether the field has constructed the intellectual foundation and practice methods considered prerequisite to achieving full status as a profession. This skepticism was expressed most notably by Abraham Flexner in his discussion of the question, "Is social work a profession?" at the National Conference of Charities and Corrections in 1915. Flexner argued that a profession must possess six traits: intellectuality, with individual responsibility; a learned character; practicality; an educationally communicable technique; a tendency to self-organization; and altruistic motivation. He concluded that in many respects (particularly with regard to individual responsibility and educationally communicable techniques), social work did not (in 1915) qualify as a profession.[13] Though we are certainly much less inclined today to question its status as a profession, it can be argued that this doubt, which persisted for many years, served to encourage practitioners and social work educators to spend their time attempting to make firmer the foundation of the profession, its tools, and techniques, rather than to pay close attention to normative issues which, by raising questions about the ethical nature of social work's mission and methods, might have appeared to threaten social work's chances of being admitted to the coterie of bona fide professions.

Finally, most social workers are employed by public or private agencies. As a a result, agency rules, regulations, and policies have frequently taken precedence over personal and professional codes of ethics and appear to have suppressed the need for many workers to systematically explore ethical guidelines for practice. This too is a somewhat conjectural thesis, but it may help to explain in part the relative lack of explicit attention that social work has paid to ethical issues and formal instruction on this subject.

D. Ethics in Contemporary Social Work

We have learned since the inauguration of social work that the field is filled with important questions of ethics and that it is important for practitioners to be sensitive to them. Though we have to some extent lagged behind several other professions in our pursuit of these questions, it is clear that social workers are beginning to generate more interest in and concern about ethical aspects of the practice of social work. It appears, in particular, that educators are coming to recognize the importance of acquainting students of social work with the nature of ethical dilemmas known to arise in practice. For example, a recent draft of the new Curriculum Policy Statement developed by the Commission on Educational Planning of the Council on Social Work Education states that:

> Identifiable consideration of values and ethical issues should be infused throughout the curriculum, including the field experience. The infusion should be such that there is the opportunity for students to acquire specific knowledge of primary and instrumental values and their ethical implications, and to test their application in practice. The aim of teaching-learning in this area is for students to develop awareness of their personal values and to be prepared to undertake work on conflicting values and ethical dilemmas.[14]

This is a noble prescription. Yet, if it is to be regarded as more than a rhetorical statement of lofty ideals, much more work needs to be done before we can meet its mandate.[15] The literature at present available on social work ethics, which is useful for teaching purposes, is limited, though it is beginning to expand. The number of courses currently devoted to social work ethics in our training programs is few.[16] If we are going to make a serious effort to introduce content on social work ethics into our curricula, we must begin to think carefully about the substantive topics that should be addressed in the teaching of social work ethics, the educational goals that should guide our instruction, pedagogical approaches, and instructor qualifications and training. We turn now to a consideration of these issues.

II. Substantive Issues in Social Work Ethics

If we hope to increase the amount of attention paid to social work ethics, it will be important for social work educators to develop a firm grasp of the range of ethical issues in the profession. Though most social work educators have some sense of the ethical problems that have been known to emerge in practice, relatively few have been exposed to an analysis of these problems from a point of view of the principles of ethics and the variety of perspectives contained within moral philosophy. It seems important to us, then, to outline the range of ethical issues we believe ought to be addressed in the teaching of social work ethics. Although our outline is not exhaustive, it includes a broad survey of the most pressing ethical issues in social work ethics.

A. Issues of Normative and Applied Ethics

In our judgment, the teaching of social work ethics should include (1) a systematic analysis of ethical principles, values, and issues that are germane to the profession, and (2) an examination of cases that illustrate the kinds of ethical dilemmas practitioners encounter in their day-to-day work. These are obviously tasks that are meant to overlap to a considerable degree; for example, discussion about an actual ethical dilemma will undoubtedly benefit from references to principles of ethics and various schools of thought within moral philosophy and social work, and discussion of abstract ethical ideas, values, and principles will ordinarily be enriched by illustrations drawn from actual cases.

The ethical dilemmas and issues that need to be addressed in social work can be placed into three broad categories: those that involve (1) services to individuals, families, and other groups (what is ordinarily referred to as direct practice); (2) the design and implementation of social welfare policies and programs; and (3) relationships among professional colleagues. We will briefly discuss the ethical dilemmas and issues in each of these areas.

1. Services to Individuals, Families, and Groups

Social workers encounter a wide variety of ethical issues and dilemmas in their work with individuals, families, and other groups. Unfortunately, it is not possible to provide here a thorough listing of these issues and dilemmas; we can, however, briefly review a number that seem to us to be among the most frequent and important.

a. *Confidentiality*. Among the most enduring of ethical principles in social work has been that concerning the issue of confidentiality. It has long been assumed that the content of discussion between a social worker and his or her client is to be held in strictest confidence by the practitioner, both out of respect for the client's privacy and to enhance the client's trust in the worker. According to the current Code of Ethics of the National Association of Social Workers, "The social worker should respect the privacy of clients and hold in confidence all information obtained in the course of professional service."

Although there is little question that this is a principle by which social workers ordinarily ought to abide, it is generally conceded that instances can arise that would require social workers to report confidential information to a third party, against a client's wishes. A social worker whose client has sincerely (and in confidence) threatened to seriously injure another person would certainly have the responsibility to alert appropriate authorities. However, there are many cases in social work that are not nearly so clear-cut. For example, is a child welfare worker always obligated to report an isolated incident of child abuse which a client has informed him about? What is a social worker's obligation when he or she has discovered that a husband has violated an agreement which he and his wife agreed to during the course of family therapy? Does that wife have a right to the truth, even if the husband refuses to reveal it to her? It is thus important for social workers to think carefully about the nature of circumstances that would warrant the disclosure of confidential information.[17]

b. *Truth-telling*. A related value, which social workers have traditionally endorsed, concerns the obligation to be truthful in their dealings with clients. We ordinarily believe that clients have a right to the truth in matters that directly concern them. But this too is a value that many practitioners believe admits of exceptions.

Whether or not it is ever permissible to lie to or withhold the truth from another person is an age-old controversy. An extreme position on this issue is that one should never lie, and that no circumstances excuse lying. According to Immanuel Kant, for example, "Truthfulness in statements which cannot be avoided is the formal duty of an individual to everyone, however great may be the disadvantage accruing to himself or to another."[18] However, others argue that circumstances can arise that would justify lying; adherents of this point of view maintain that it is foolish to obey a principle such as "never lie" when a particular lie could result in a greater good or would prevent harm that would result from telling the truth. Should a suicidal client who has asked for a candid assessment of his condition be told the truth if the social worker believes that the truth might push the client over the edge? Does a hospital social worker have an obligation to tell a dying patient the truth about her prognosis even though family members have asked the practitioner not to do so? Does a social worker who is serving as a drug abuse counselor have an obligation to share the doubts he has about one of his clients with a prospective employer who has asked for a letter of reference regarding the client? Social workers certainly need to be made aware of the various arguments that have been presented for and against the need to tell the truth.[19]

c. *Paternalism and Self-Determination*. Social workers are ordinarily attracted to the profession because of their desire to assist people who are experiencing problems in living. Prospective practitioners attend schools of social work in order to become acquainted with and master methods of helping. There is little doubt that in many instances the various interventions that social workers design and implement are both important and appropriate. They frequently respond to the genuine needs of people who have significant problems. On occasion, however, serious questions can be raised about the propriety of social workers' interventions. One important question is related to acts of paternalism, that is, where a professional intervenes in a client's life against his or her own wishes on the grounds that it is for the client's own good that the social worker intervenes. The extent to which professionals have a right to intervene in a fashion contrary to client's wishes (for example, by reporting self-destructive behavior to mental health authorities, or by trying to talk a client out of a decision he or she has made about a particular course of action) has been debated for decades and is not likely to be settled easily.[20] The debate about the limits of paternalism is relevant to social workers who work with clients privately, as well as to practitioners who represent public agencies.

Questions concerning paternalism raise, in turn, important questions about a concept that has been central to social work for decades: self-determination. A traditional assumption in social work has been that clients have a fundamental right to self-determination which practitioners are obligated to respect. According to the NASW Code of Ethics, "The social worker should make every effort to foster maximum self-determination on the part of the client."[21] An extreme interpretation of this principle runs directly counter to acts of paternalism where social workers intervene in a manner opposed by the client. According to a strict interpretation of the principle of self-determination, clients should be permitted to pursue their own goals with whatever means they wish to employ. They have a right to what Sir Isaiah Berlin has referred to as "negative liberty," that is, the right to be left alone and not to be coerced.[22]

As social workers we are ordinarily inclined to respect a client's choice of goals and the paths which a client has chosen in order to reach those goals. It is commonly assumed that clients should not only have their preferences honored, but that social work is likely to be ineffective when a practitioner pursues goals a client neither endorses nor embraces. Most of us, however, recognize that extreme circumstances can arise when, deep down inside, we believe that a client is not acting in his or her own best interests and must be interfered with and denied the right to self-determination. The difficulty, of course, is in identifying and agreeing upon the nature of circumstances that warrant such paternalistic interference. Whereas many practitioners would agree that we ought to intervene when, in a sudden fit of depression, a client attempts to commit suicide, we are less inclined to agree when we address more ambiguous cases (for example, whether we have the right to interfere with a mildly retarded client who has decided to try to conceive a child, or with an individual who has chosen to live in conditions that strike many of us as abhorrent). Important questions related to the client's right to self-determination also arise in instances when the client's values conflict with the social worker's. For example, how assertive should a worker be when a client espouses and acts in accord with values that are clearly racist, sexist, or otherwise discriminatory or morally repugnant?

d. *Adherence to Laws, Policies, and Regulations*. A recurring dilemma in social work concerns the obligation of practitioners to obey laws, policies, and regulations. We ordinarily assume that social workers are obliged to act in accord with established laws, policies, and regulations; for example, practitioners generally agree that it is wrong to falsify one's credentials, which in most states would be a violation of law, in order to obtain employment or attract clients, and that it would be wrong to violate an agency policy concerning the release of confidential information. Yet many social workers claim that circumstances can arise that would obligate them to violate a law, rule, or regulation. For example, practitioners have been known to violate a state law that requires the reporting of any case of suspected child abuse on the ground that staff of the state protective services unit are so incompetent that they would do more harm than good, or that reporting the suspected abuse would threaten the worker's therapeutic relationship with the client. The justification in such cases is ordinarily that the greatest good with respect to the client's well-being will most likely result from not obeying the law, policy, or regulation.

Whether or not this is ever an acceptable argument is highly debatable. On the one hand, there is the point of view that "the law is the law" and that professionals have an obligation to obey it, whether or not they approve of its particular content.[23] Adherents of this position claim that to allow individuals to use their discretion in deciding whether a law ought to be obeyed invites social chaos and a legal charade in which laws would have no teeth (or would at best have dentures, which could be inserted for bite in response to one's preferences, whims, and convenience!). Opponents of this point of view claim, as one would expect, that it is a mistake to obey a law, policy, or regulation when not doing so would result in a greater good or would prevent serious harm; that is, one value (such as preventing injury to others) can override another (such as obeying a law) when the former is of a "higher order," results in a greater good, or prevents more harm. They argue that professionals have an obligation to protect and enhance the welfare of clients and, on occasion, this obligation may require one to violate a law, policy, or regulation in order to avoid the damaging (and unnecessary, they would assert) consequences of what the philosopher J. J. C. Smart has referred to as "rule worship."[24]

e. *Divided Professional Loyalties.* A long-standing assumption in social work is that the practitioner's primary obligation is to respond to the needs of clients. There is little question that the success of the casework relationship depends to a significant extent on the client's belief that the social worker is in his or her corner, and is someone who will advocate for the client through thick and thin. The NASW Code of Ethics asserts, in fact, that, "The social worker's primary responsibility is to clients."

Difficult problems can arise, however, when a social worker feels caught between the obligation to act in accord with the needs of one's client and the pressing needs of others. Such conflicts can arise in a variety of ways. On occasion, for example, a social worker can find him or herself caught between a client's needs and interests and the needs and interests of the client's relatives or acquaintances. A worker whose client has threatened to harm psychologically a relative or acquaintance must choose between supporting the client and protecting the threatened third party, perhaps at the expense of the client. Another conflict can arise between the needs and interests of one's client and the needs and interests of one's own agency. Is it permissible for a practitioner to violate an agency policy which prohibits social workers from treating clients privately when a particular client is suffering deeply and requires more assistance than can be provided during agency hours? Is it permissible for a social worker to provide furtive assistance to an indigent client who cannot afford the fee for service, even though doing so is contrary to agency policy? Thus, the social worker's obligation to act primarily in accord with the client's needs and interests must sometimes be reconciled with the obligation stated in the NASW Code of Ethics that, "The social worker should adhere to commitments made to the employing organization." Similar conflicts can also arise when the needs and interests of one's client clash with the needs and interests of other agencies or organizations, such as a court of law, a public social service agency, or law enforcement officials. Social workers need to consider the nature of circumstances which may, in rare instances, warrant placing the interests of others above those of one's clients.

f. *Distribution of Limited Resources.* Social workers who provide services directly to individuals, families, and other groups are frequently in a position to distribute resources that are in limited supply. Sometimes these are tangible resources—such as social service funds, bed space in an emergency shelter, and equipment—and sometimes they are intangible—such as the amount of time and attention available for clients.

It is important for social workers to consider carefully the criteria used to distribute scarce resources. It is frequently tempting, for example, to distribute goods and resources based on the principle of equality, but we must recognize that this is an ambiguous concept which is subject to a variety of interpretations. To some it implies that goods and resources should be divided equally among eligible recipients, so that each receives an equal share. To others, the concept of equality implies only equality of opportunity, such that all eligible recipients are provided with an equal chance to receive goods and resources, based either on a principle of first-come-first-served, or on a lottery or random drawing. Of course, some goods and resources, such as shelter beds, cannot be divided among eligible users equally if the demand exceeds the supply; others, such as social service funds, can—at least in principle—be divided equally among eligible recipients.[25]

Some practitioners would argue that some limited goods and resources should not be distributed according to the principle of equality, in any of its forms, but should be distributed instead on the basis of need. Thus, according to adherents of this point of view, social service funds and worker time and attention should be dispensed to those who demonstrate the greatest need for them rather than to everyone equally or on the basis of a lottery. Still others argue that it is justifiable to distribute goods and resources based on the extent of eligible recipients' past contributions, in a manner that compensates for past injustices, or to those who are most likely to benefit. For example, it is sometimes argued that individuals who have done much to enhance the quality of life of a community should be catered to in emergency situations before those who have contributed less or who have been a drain on community resources. It is also not unusual to hear social workers argue that descendents of groups that were subjected to abuse and discrimination in the past have a greater claim to certain goods and resources (for example, jobs or admission to colleges and universities) than do others, in order to compensate for past misdeeds. Finally, it is also frequently argued that limited goods and resources should be distributed to those individuals who will most likely benefit from them, in accord with the principle of triage. Clearly, the criteria used to distribute limited goods and resources, and the reasons that lie behind their use, require careful attention.

2. Social Welfare Policy and Programs

Social workers also encounter a wide variety of ethical issues and dilemmas related to the design and implementation of social welfare policies and programs. We will identify and briefly discuss those issues that seem particularly deserving of attention in the teaching of social work.

a. *Welfare Rights.* For centuries there has been considerable debate about the extent of society's obligation to care for the needy. Controversy surrounding the Elizabethan Poor Law of 1601—which was designed in part to respond to the needs of vulnerable children and the disabled—and the English Poor Law

Reform Bill of 1834—which, in the spirit of the laissez-faire economics of Adam Smith and David Ricardo, ended public assistance for ablebodied persons (except in public institutions)—represent milestones in this persistent debate about the rights destitute individuals have to public support and subsidy. The sides of the debate have been clearly drawn for ages. On the one hand, there are those who assume that many people are poor for reasons beyond their control, such as illness, age, family status, or some other disabling condition, and that these individuals have a fundamental right to care provided at public expense. On the other side of the debate are those who claim that a large proportion of those who receive public assistance are ablebodied and avoid gainful employment only because they are lazy and shiftless.

A practical consequence of this debate is that in many communities around the country programs have been devised that require the ablebodied poor to work for the community in some capacity in exchange for welfare benefits. These so-called "workfare" programs have been designed with several goals in mind: (1) to discourage the ablebodied poor from applying for welfare benefits; (2) to reduce the costs of local public assistance programs; and (3) to respond to the resentment of community residents who feel that they are supporting unworthy poor. Many of these workfare programs threaten to terminate benefits for recipients who refuse to work in exchange for the assistance they receive. The merits of such programs are widely debated, illustrating the obstinacy of controversy about the rights poor people have to public assistance.

b. *The Role of the State.* An issue closely related to the concept of welfare rights concerns the involvement of the state—in the form of federal, state, and local government—in welfare matters. Many social workers are inclined to believe that units of government are obligated to provide for certain basic welfare needs of individuals who are poor, disabled, elderly, or otherwise unable to adequately care for themselves. Social workers, in fact, have been instrumental in attempts to design and implement large-scale social service programs operated under government auspices, including programs such as Social Security, Medicaid, Medicare, Food Stamps, and many other programs operated at state and local levels that are intended to address problems such as crime and delinquency, inferior education, unemployment, mental illness, and inadequate child care.

It is important for social workers to recognize that there is considerable disagreement about the extent to which units of government ought to be involved in social welfare matters through the funding or sponsoring of programs. Debates about national health insurance, government funding of abortions, the subsidizing of job-training programs or day care, and other such programs and policies illustrate the level of disagreement.

Controversy related to the involvement of government has persisted for centuries, though much modern debate has its roots in the nineteenth-century conflict between the doctrine of laissez-faire—which decried government involvement in private enterprise—and mercantilism—which advocated government regulation, protective tariffs, and other policies designed to promote economic health.[26] In fact, the expansion of the state's role in welfare matters can be largely attributed to a decline in confidence following the Great European Depression of the 1870s in the ability of a free market to provide for and sustain individual welfare. The fundamental differences between the views of Presidents Jimmy Carter and Ronald Reagan about the merits of government-sponsored social welfare programs, as opposed to social services that are generated out of the concerns of private citizens and the invisible hand of the unregulated (or minimally regulated) market, demonstrate the persistence and salience of this important ethical question.

c. *Distributive Justice.* In our discussion of ethical problems that arise in direct practice with individuals and families, we observed that circumstances sometimes require social workers to make difficult choices concerning the distribution of limited resources. Such dilemmas are also encountered by social workers who have responsibility for the design and implementation of social welfare policies and programs. For example, important questions related to distributive justice arise whenever decisions are made about income maintenance and public assistance programs. Conclusions reached about minimum guaranteed incomes, criteria for establishing poverty levels, and levels of taxation rest on assumptions about how wealth ought to be distributed among citizens. Similarly, judgments about funding priorities and the criteria that should be used to distribute limited funds to competing groups depend upon assumptions about the rights members of various groups have to assistance and the criteria that should be used to determine when one group should be favored over another. For instance, individuals who favor distributing limited resources on the basis of need may have very different opinions about how federal funds for vocational rehabilitation programs or general assistance funds should be distributed from those of individuals who favor a principle of equality. The ways in which we operationalize our definitions of concepts such as need, equality, and so on can have profound consequences for the ways in which goods and resources are allocated or made accessible to individuals and groups through social welfare policies and programs.

Questions regarding distributive justice are closely related to social work's traditional mission in Western capitalistic nations. Prevailing ideology in the United States and in other Western nations has important consequences for the persistence of poverty and unemployment, and the allocation of income; social workers need to be encouraged to examine critically the economic and political underpinnings of the world in which they work and the extent to which they are willing to accept the status quo or advocate for social change.

d. *Social Injustice and Professional Priorities.* Social workers have traditionally assumed responsibility for assisting individuals who have suffered various forms of discrimination, harsh treatment, or who have otherwise fallen through the safety net provided by existing social welfare policies and programs. It is important for social work educators to routinely, systematically, and conscientiously expose prospective practitioners to the nagging problems of racism, sexism, and the disturbing side effects of life in a nation that relies to a considerable extent on the free market to produce economic and social well-being.

One of the most important decisions every social worker needs to make concerns the amount of time he or she will devote to advocating for social change and reform as opposed to therapy and work with individual clients. A related issue concerns the clients with whom social workers choose to work. In the early

years of the profession, for example, social workers were preoccupied with problems of the poor. Today, however, social workers serve a much larger number of client populations, including
the elderly, disabled, infirm, mentally disturbed, criminal, and
abandoned. Many of us are inclined to applaud social workers'
efforts to serve these various populations and to address the wide
variety of problems in living from which people suffer. It is
important to acknowledge, however, that there is substantial resentment within the profession about the extent to which and the
directions in which social work's boundaries have expanded.
There is some belief within the profession, for example, that
many social workers have largely abandoned their commitment to
the poor and have chosen instead to work with more affluent
clients. In particular, some practitioners complain vociferously
about the amount of time that some social workers are spending
in private practice serving clients who can afford the expense of
private psychotherapy.

Whether or not social workers have inappropriately gravitated
toward work with relatively affluent populations at the expense of
the least advantaged and social reform is highly debatable, and it
is a controversy that cannot be settled easily. We believe, however, that instruction on the subject of social work ethics should
address this topic of professional priorities and the nature of
social workers' obligations to people in need.

3. Dilemmas Among Professional Colleagues

The third area in which social workers encounter ethical dilemmas is related to their relationships with professional colleagues.
These dilemmas concern the nature of social workers' obligations
in instances when they become aware of wrongdoing engaged in
by colleagues, the use of deception in practice, the nature of
social workers' right to privileged communication, and ethical
dilemmas that arise in work with interdisciplinary teams.

a. *Whistle-blowing*. It is not uncommon for practitioners to
become aware periodically of colleagues who are engaging in or
have engaged in some form of wrongdoing or indiscretion. In
social work such wrongdoing can assume a variety of forms,
ranging from violating an agency regulation or law, submitting

bogus travel vouchers, presenting false credentials, overcharging clients, or otherwise abusing clients.

It is frequently difficult for social workers to decide what their responsibility is in such cases. On the one hand it may seem that social workers should report wrongdoing whenever it appears to seriously threaten the well-being of clients or other individuals. But is this always the case? Suppose one stands to lose one's job or to be severely disciplined (directly or indirectly) because one has "blown the whistle" on a colleague. Does this change the nature of a practitioner's obligation to report wrongdoing? Suppose the colleague who is engaged in wrongdoing is a close friend. How does this affect the nature of one's professional responsibility?

Blowing the whistle on a colleague can obviously have serious consequences, both for the colleague and the whistle-blower. These cases provide an additional example of ethical dilemmas in social work that require practitioners to balance the rights of well-being of clients and other vulnerable individuals with the well-being of one's colleagues and one's self. Unfortunately, professionals have not had clear guidelines concerning whistle-blowing and the conflicts of interest that arise in such cases. As Sissela Bok has observed: "It is rare to find a case in which all factors support the sounding of a public alarm to disclose impropriety in one's organization: where the cause is just; where less dramatic alternatives have been exhausted; where responsibility is openly accepted; where the whistleblower is above reproach."[27] It is thus important for social workers to carefully consider the nature of circumstances that seem to call for whistle-blowing and those that call for less drastic responses.[28]

b. *The Use of Deception.* Social workers ordinarily oppose the use of deceptive practices during the course of their professional activities. As a general principle, practitioners tend to oppose the deliberate withholding of information that is important to other people, lying, the breaking of promises, and so on. Instances do arise, however, that lead some practitioners to believe that it is permissible to engage in the use of deception. For example, in a large midwestern city, a watchdog organization recently obtained information that suggested that residents in a state institution for the mentally retarded were being physically abused by several staff members. The organization arranged to film activities in the institution, without the knowledge of the institution's staff or residents, in order to document the alleged abuses. While some people objected to the surreptitious methods used, the investigation and filming were widely acclaimed on the grounds that they were necessary in order to reveal the reprehensible abuses that were taking place within the institution.

In a second case, staff of a watchdog organization used false credentials and identities in order to gain employment as nurses' aides in several abortion clinics that were reportedly using illegal and nonprofessional procedures on their patients. Was the use of deception in these cases justified by the danger that clients were apparently being subjected to? What distinctions should we make between the use of deception in order to obtain a job, overcharge clients, or evade income taxes, and the use of deception in order to protect clients who are apparently being subjected to abuse? It is important for practitioners to think carefully about the use of deception in their relationships with colleagues and the nature of circumstances that might, in extreme instances, justify its use.[29]

c. *Privileged Communication.* As we noted earlier, social workers generally assume that information shared by clients should be kept confidential, both in order to respect the client's right to privacy and to enhance the client's faith in the trustworthiness of his or her worker. It occasionally happens, however, that a practitioner or agency worker will be called upon by a professional colleague to disclose information that a client has shared in confidence. A fellow social worker employed by another agency that is also serving the client (for example, a hospital or school social worker) may request information he or she believes is necessary in order to adequately serve the client. A social worker may also be requested by law-enforcement authorities or court officials, either formally or by means of a subpoena, to disclose confidential information without the client's permission.

Ordinarily, social workers believe that they should share information with others only with the client's permission. There are some instances, however, when social workers believe that no harm is done, that harm can be prevented, or that it is actually in the client's best interest when the worker shares information with a professional colleague. For example, some practitioners might consider it important and appropriate for a school social worker to share his or her impressions with a private practitioner who is working with a child who is having difficulties in the classroom. Similarly, many practitioners consider it appropriate for a social worker to reveal information to a supervisor who is providing consultation on a particular case. It is important to recognize that social workers disagree about the appropriateness of revealing information shared by a client with others, especially without the client's permission. Is a social worker who is in private practice obligated to reveal information to an officer of the court who wants information about a client's personality attributes and parenting abilities in order to resolve a custody dispute? Should a social worker always disclose information to law-enforcement officials about a client's allegedly illegal activities? What is the nature of a social worker's obligation to reveal confidential information which has been subpoenaed by a court of law?[30]

d. *Interdisciplinary Conflicts.* Social workers have been involved in interdisciplinary work with other professions in health, mental health, court, and school settings for decades. Interdisciplinary collaboration is ordinarily viewed as a sensible way to coordinate a variety of services for clients whose problems and needs call for assistance from members of several professions. It is well known, however, that interdisciplinary work can give rise periodically to confusion and disagreement regarding treatment goals, responsibilities, treatment procedures, lines of communication, and interpersonal relations. Such circumstances can present social workers (and other professionals) with difficult ethical dilemmas.

The value and ethical conflicts which social workers involved in interdisciplinary work face are determined in part by the client population being served, the nature of the social worker's responsibilities, organizational procedures and mechanisms for collaboration among professionals, and by the responsibilities of the professionals with whom the social worker is teamed. For example, clients who are poor, vulnerable, or otherwise disadvantaged often need someone to advocate for their rights. When social workers engage in advocacy in order to secure or protect the rights of clients in a manner that runs counter to team decisions, sentiments, or standard operating procedures, their relationships with other team members may be jeopardized. A social worker who argues that an elderly nursing home resident has a right to seek medical care from the physician of her choice rather than be required to receive care from the nursing home's resident physician faces a choice between the rights of her client and established nursing home policy. A hospital social worker who argues that a terminally ill patient has a right to be informed about his condition when other members of the health-care team disagree must also make a difficult choice between the right she believes the patient has to know about his condition and the preferences of her professional colleagues. A related problem can emerge when another team member, such as a nurse, doctor, or teacher, wishes to assume responsibility for service that the social worker believes is her responsibility to perform because of her particular training and skills. Here, too, the social worker may have to make a difficult choice about the need to challenge the intentions of professional colleagues. These dilemmas can be complicated even further when a social worker is employed in a setting in which members of the other professions with which one collaborates have greater administrative authority; this is particularly so for social workers employed in health-care settings.[31]

Thus far we have described the range of ethical issues that social workers have been known to encounter in their work with individuals, families, and groups, in the design and implementation of social welfare policies and programs, and in their relationships with professional colleagues. It is important for social workers to have an appreciation of the variety of ethical issues and dilemmas encountered in practice; it is equally important for them to be acquainted with the various schools of thought that have developed over the centuries as to how ethical issues and dilemmas should be analyzed and resolved. This brings us to a consideration of issues of metaethics, that is, issues concerning the meaning of ethical terms, the justification of values, and the derivation of ethical principles and guidelines.

B. Issues of Metaethics

Debate about ways of analyzing and resolving ethical issues and dilemmas has endured for centuries in moral philosophy. Controversy has stemmed in part from disagreement about whether it is even possible to derive ethical principles (such as "Don't lie"; "Keep a promise"; and "Don't harm others") that represent more than individual opinion, intuition, or sentiments about what is right and wrong, good and bad. That is, there are those who argue that absolute standards of morality or principles of ethics that would be considered applicable to all people can neither be derived nor known, and that principles of ethics reflect nothing more than our opinions about what is right and wrong, good and bad. According to these so-called relativists, what we consider to be right and wrong, and good and bad, therefore depends upon, for example, our cultural heritage or traditions, religious preferences and beliefs, political affiliations, or other influences that reflect circumstances that may change over time and that may vary from locale to locale. Thus, relativists hold that absolute moral standards that can be shown to hold for all people at all times—that is, regardless of one's religion, politics, geographical location, or era—simply do not exist, and that ethical statements are merely a function of one's personal circumstances, feelings, and opinions.[32]

Support for the relativist's position has waxed and waned over time, along with concern about moral standards generally. Tolerance for relativism has tended to coincide, historically, with periods of skepticism concerning orthodox religion, particularly Christian monotheism. In recent years, however, the popularity of ethical relativism seems to have declined, with an accompanying increase of interest in the development of moral standards, as if to serve as a ballast during uncertain and precarious times. There appears to be less patience generally for a moral philosophy that permits a very wide variety of standards of behavior. This trend seems to characterize social work as well. The relatively recent surge of interest in deriving ethical guidelines for the profession contrasts sharply with the mood of the 1960s, which was perhaps the era in recent history that was most conducive to the growth of relativism. The extent to which values and ethical issues *can* in fact be derived and justified or shown to be true is thus an important subject to address in social work education. Are there certain values that we believe apply to all people in all places and at all times? How willing are we to tolerate differences in clients' and colleagues' opinions about what constitutes mental health, social security, welfare, non-discrimination, freedom, and justice?

I. Social Work and Metaethics

For many years social workers have espoused a variety of values that are intended to guide and inform the behavior of practitioners, including the client's right to self-determination, fairness, equality, individual dignity and choice, justice, freedom, well-being, and so forth.[33] The profession has also developed and revised several codes of ethics in an attempt to prescribe ethical and proscribe unethical behavior. Until relatively recently, introducing prospective social workers to traditional values of the profession and to the Code of Ethics was frequently carried out in an almost perfunctory manner, with less-than-rigorous discussion of the ethical dilemmas that can arise in practice. We have slowly come to realize, however, that contemporary social work is rife with difficult and frequently perplexing ethical dilemmas that call for careful and informed judgment. We have grown less and less satisfied with the *prima facie* assertion of values and ethical principles that has tended to characterize the profession and are moving toward the careful consideration of questions regarding the meaning of ethical terms (for example: What exactly do we mean by terms such as altruism, welfare, mental health, equality, or self-determination? What behavior constitutes *good* behavior in the moral sense?) and ways of justifying and deriving values and ethical principles (for example: What place do religious beliefs and science have in the determination of what is right or wrong?). Perhaps the most pressing metaethical question that needs to be addressed by social workers concerns ways of reconciling conflicts among values.

2. Conflicts Among Values

Ordinarily we have little difficulty agreeing that certain values ought to be adhered to in the practice of social work. There is general agreement that information shared by clients ordinarily ought to be kept confidential, that social workers ought to promote a client's self-determination, that social workers should not lie to or deceive their clients, and so on. The cases and circumstances with which we struggle, rather, are primarily those that require choices between and among values which, considered individually, we are inclined to adhere to. For example, a social worker whose client has thoughtfully planned to injure himself must decide between the value of a client's right to self-determination and of protecting the client's well-being. A social worker whose client has apparently abused his child must choose between the value of confidentiality and of obeying a law that requires practitioners to report suspected cases of abuse. A community organizer who has been asked by her constituents to advocate for a housing ordinance designed to inhibit the movement of minorities into ·the neighborhood must choose between her obligation to oppose discrimination (as stated in the NASW Code of Ethics) and her commitment to advocate for the community she represents. These are the difficult cases, where statements of isolated values and broad principles of ethics frequently leave one stranded with a difficult choice among values.

Philosophers have had a variety of opinions about how one should choose among competing values. Some have argued that certain values, laws, or rules are inherently right or good and should be adhered to, regardless of the consequences (proponents of this point of view are generally referred to as deontologists).[34] Others have argued that ethical choices should be guided by an assessment of consequences, that is, that the rightness of an act is determined by the goodness of its consequences (adherents of this point of view are generally referred to as teleologists).[35] Perhaps the most popular version of this latter point of view is utilitarianism which, in its simplest form, is interpreted to mean that those acts should be engaged in which produce the greatest balance of good over evil. According to the English jurist and philosopher, Jeremy Bentham, the consequences of actions should be estimated by considering seven dimensions: certainty, duration, intensity, propinquity, fecundity, purity, and extent. John Stuart Mill later introduced qualitative considerations as well, making distinctions amoung "higher" and "lower" pleasures, and more and less important duties, in his classic essay, *Utilitarianism*.

While many important arguments have been developed for and against deontological and utilitarian principles as ways of approaching ethical dilemmas (arguments with which the teaching of social work ethics should acquaint students),[36] there is considerable agreement among moral philosophers that it is important to construct a hierarchy of values, such that in cases of conflict certain values are considered to take precedence over others. Thus, one might argue that in cases of conflict, one person's right to well-being takes precedence over another person's right to confidentiality, if the former's welfare can be protected only by the release of confidential information. Or, one might argue that the right of a group of mentally retarded individuals to humane care in a noninstitutional setting takes precedence over a community's right to oppose the location of a group home in the neighborhood, or that equality of opportunity is more important than actual equality in cases of conflict. Though there is considerable disagreement among philosophers about the ways in which such a hierarchy (or what John Rawls refers to as a "lexical ordering")[37] should be derived, it is important that instruction on social work ethics directly address this topic. The choices we make when confronted with ethical dilemmas where two or more values conflict frequently rest on a hierarchy of values that we adhere to implicitly or explicitly.

As we noted earlier, it is important for social workers to have some familiarity with questions of metaethics—questions about the meaning of ethical terms and ways of deriving and justifying ethical principles. Throughout the history of the profession, we have tended to assume that the values we have traditionally adhered to have inherent validity. Raising questions of metaethics can assist social workers to examine critically the content and origins of their values and ethical beliefs and the criteria used to choose among competing values.

III. Teaching Social Work Ethics

Thus far we have concentrated on an outline of substantive issues that we believe should be addressed in the teaching of social work ethics. We turn now to a discussion of teaching approaches and ways of presenting material related to social work ethics.

As we noted earlier, the general subject of social work values and ethics has been addressed for some time in schools of social work.[38] As we also noted, however, the number of courses currently devoted to social work ethics nationwide is relatively small, though many schools offer courses that include sections devoted to the subject of values and ethics. It is clear that at present the subject of social work ethics is not a standard component of most social work curricula. Nonetheless, it is also evident that interest in social work ethics among educators in the profession is growing. Moreover, the prescription in the most recent draft of the revised Curriculum Policy Statement of the Council on Social Work Education, concerning the need to systematically include this subject in the profession's curricula, has given even further impetus to the growth of interest in the teaching of social work ethics. It is therefore important that social work educators be encouraged to think carefully about the goals of teaching social work ethics, pedagogical approaches and teaching techniques, course content, and instructor qualifications.

A. Educational Goals

Courses on the subject of professional ethics have had a variety of goals. Some courses have concentrated on attempting to help students identify and assess ethical issues and dilemmas, with an emphasis on acquainting students with the analytical tools that moral philosophers have developed over the years. Others have stressed what has come to be known as "values clarification," that is, having students struggle critically with their own inchoate or well-entrenched values. Our own view concerning the proper goals of instruction on social work ethics coincides with conclusions reached in The Hastings Center Report, *The Teaching of Ethics in Higher Education*: "We believe that the primary purpose of courses in ethics ought to be to provide students with those concepts and analytical skills that will enable them to grapple with broad ethical theory in attempting to resolve both personal and professional dilemmas, as well as to reflect on the moral issues facing the larger society."[39] More specifically, courses on the subject of social work ethics should focus on:

1. Stimulating the Moral Imagination

Professional education in social work primarily entails instruction on methods and techniques of assisting people, including diagnostic and counseling techniques, community organization skills, strategies of policy formulation, and so on. In addition, social work education tends to acquaint students with knowledge of human development, social welfare history, and methods of research. A relatively small percentage of social work education is devoted to acquainting students with the ethical problems encountered by practitioners, their characteristics, and ways of identifying them. It is important to help students learn to recognize ethical issues and dilemmas in social work and to think systematically about them. Time needs to be given to the ethical aspects of social work as well as to the art and science of social work. It is also important for practitioners to appreciate that mastery of social work practice skills and techniques alone will not necessarily enable one to respond adequately to the difficult and frequently painful ethical choices individuals encounter and the profound feelings and anguish that people caught in the midst of such dilemmas are at times burdened by.

2. Developing Analytical Skills

The cognitive skills that social work educators attempt to help students cultivate regarding the "technical" aspects of social work are not significantly different from the cognitive skills a moral philosopher brings to bear on problems of ethics. There is considerable consensus among educators in all fields and disciplines that the use of the canons of inductive and deductive logic, the ability to recognize fallacies, and other traits of rational thought are prerequisite to the careful analysis of any problem. Discussions about values and ethics, and about the beliefs we hold concerning what is right and wrong, or good and bad, are often emotionally charged; although it is important that we not extract or drain our feelings from such discussions (to do so would render them both sterile and artificial), it is important that students and educators hold one another to principles of rational discourse and debate. Sound judgments about ethical dilemmas require sound reasoning.

As we observed earlier, moral philosophers have speculated for centuries about what constitutes right and wrong, and good and bad. It is also important for social workers to become acquainted with the traditional schools of thought on ethical matters, and with the arguments in support of and opposed to these various points of view. It is useful for practitioners to consider the merits of *what* moral philosophers have argued in addition to the merits of the *ways* in which they have presented their arguments.

3. Eliciting a Sense of Moral Obligation and Personal Responsibility

A variety of factors influence the decisions that social workers make in practice. We tend to be influenced by the intervention methods we were exposed to during our training, by the techniques used by esteemed supervisors and colleagues, by the theoretical assertions of social work educators and practitioners, and by the results of research on social work phenomena. In addition, of course, our decisions in practice are also influenced by more personal factors, such as the personal appeal of the individuals with whom we have contact, the enjoyment we experience as a result of providing certain forms of help, and the preferences we have for ways of spending our time off of the job.

In addition to these factors, however, our judgments about intervening in the lives of people also tend to be influenced by our feelings and beliefs concerning what is right and wrong, or good and bad, in a moral sense. That is, many social workers have developed strong convictions about which needs of people are among the most basic—which needs a society or community has a duty or obligation to try to meet. It is important for social workers, current and prospective, to be encouraged to think carefully and critically about the nature of moral duty and the extent of their obligation to people in need. The conclusions we reach about the moral (as opposed to the nonmoral) aspects of social work can have profound consequences for the decisions we make about the populations we choose to work with (for example, whether social workers ought primarily to serve the least advantaged), the role of government in welfare matters, the distribution of scarce resources, and the decisions we make in individual cases concerning the need to intervene and ways of intervening. All of us make moral choices in the practice of social work. It is important that we closely examine the nature of our own sense of moral responsibility and its relationship to the nonmoral (that is, technical) aspects of social work.

4. Tolerating and Resisting Disagreement and Ambiguity

Ethical issues are notorious for the amount of disagreement they can generate among interested parties. Contemporary controversies about issues such as abortion, capital punishment, and euthanasia demonstrate the volatile nature of certain ethical issues and the persistent disagreement that accompanies them. In social work, differences of opinion about, for example, how limited resources ought to be distrubuted or when it is permissible to reveal confidential information against a client's wishes, break a law, or engage in deception illustrate the extent to which disagreement and ambiguity frequently characterize discussions about ethics. There is often considerable disagreement about the very meaning of ethical terms, the derivation of ethical guidelines, and ways of applying ethical principles and values to individual ethical dilemmas.

This fact should not be taken to mean that discussions about ethics are ultimately futile and destined to be mired in intellectual disagreement, or that we ought to resign ourselves to the world of relativism. Disciplined and informed discussions of ethical issues can help practitioners clarify and challenge their own and one another's thinking. Moreover, whether or not social workers eventually reach a consensus about ethical issues as a result of their discussions, each of us must at times make personal decisions about matters of right and wrong, good and bad, and duty and obligation. Often such decisions are not made in the midst of unanimous opinion and unequivocal guidelines. It is thus important for social workers to be made aware of the disagreement and ambiguity that frequently characterize reflection on and discussion of ethical issues.

Given the controversial nature of many ethical debates, instructors must pay close attention to the effect which the communication of their own opinions can have on students. Students are impressionable at times and may look to their instructors' opinions for moral guidance. The complexity and ambiguity that are frequently associated with ethical dilemmas may serve to enhance the extent to which students look to teachers for answers. We do not believe, however, that as a result instructors must necessarily withhold their personal judgments and opinions about ethical issues in social work. On the contrary, we believe that it is important for students to observe their instructors as they too wrestle with the ethical problems of the profession and as they present their beliefs about right and wrong. This very process can often do more than the best didactic teaching to convey to students the complexity and importance of ethical issues and a sense of the ethical responsibility of professionals. We also believe, however, that instructors need to conscientiously avoid using the lectern as an opportunity to indoctrinate students. There is an important and critical difference between expressing firmly held opinions—and acknowledging them as such—and attempts to indoctrinate or proselytize. We support the conclusion reached on this topic in The Hastings Center Report on *The Teaching of Ethics in Higher Education*:

> Teachers should feel perfectly free to express their own moral convictions. At the very least, this can be helpful to students—to see how someone, who has

presumably thought more systematically and over a long period about morality, frames arguments and justifies his or her own position. But it is no less important that the teachers supply the student with those analytic tools and a range of reading matter that will enable the student to develop an independent stance. With respect to indoctrination, the test of the teaching of ethics is not whether students end by sharing the convictions of their teachers, but whether they have come to those convictions by means of the use of skills that might have led in other directions and may do so in the future.[40]

B. Teaching Techniques and Course Organization

1. Inductive v. Deductive Approaches

The teaching of applied and professional ethics has been organized and approached in a variety of ways. Many instructors in the various professions rely heavily on the use of actual cases from practice in order to illustrate ethical dilemmas generally, highlight specific ethical issues, and generate discussion among students. The principal goal of courses that are organized around the analysis of cases is to encourage students to formulate and construct general ethical principles based upon their critical examination of circumstances that arise in the individual case studies. This is an approach that is primarily inductive in design, in that it invites students to formulate general principles and guidelines following an analysis of individual cases. Thus, general principles regarding the release of confidential information or the distribution of limited resources would follow an examination of individual cases that present dilemmas on these particular subjects.

The inductive approach contrasts with an approach that begins with a review of general ethical principles and theories of ethics and then applies them to the analysis of individual cases. For example, an instructor might begin with a review of Bentham's and Mill's formulations of utilitarianism, Rawls's theory of justice, or Kant's categorical imperative, and then ask students to apply these principles to an analysis of specific cases. This is an approach that is primarily deductive in design, in that it moves from a review of general principles to an examination of individual cases.

Our experience suggests that the teaching of social work ethics should rely on both the inductive and deductive approaches. Both have merits and demerits, and instructors should do their best to draw on the strengths of each approach while avoiding their weaknesses. It is important, on the one hand, for students to have a sound appreciation of the traditions of thought in moral philosophy and of the various theories of ethics that have been devised over the centuries in order to address adequately specific ethical dilemmas. However, the experience of many instructors suggests that courses that dwell too heavily on ethical theory and subtle or esoteric issues of moral philosophy may lose students who are primarily interested in the analysis of "real" cases of the sort they are likely to encounter in practice. As Muriel Pumphrey observed in her 1959 survey of courses on social work ethics, students felt a need "to find a middle range of abstraction. They seemed to be satisfied neither with high level abstractions such as 'democracy,' 'acceptance,' and so on, nor with discussing material exclusively from the situational point of view."[41] Thus, it would also be a mistake for instructors to err in the direction of concentrating on the analysis of individual cases. Our experience suggests that the most desirable arrangement is one in which the instructor moves back and forth between the circumstances of individual cases and broader principles of ethics, weaving the two levels of analysis together as much as possible. It may be best to begin a course on social work ethics with a review of the range and types of ethical issues and dilemmas that social workers have been known to encounter in practice, followed by a review of the ways in which moral philosophers and other ethicists have approached the analysis of ethical questions (including a review of schools of thought concerning issues of metaethics and normative ethics).[42] Moving from an initial review of actual cases to a review of principles of ethics and ethical theory (and then back again) can help whet the appetites of students who might otherwise be tempted to eschew discussions based on an examination of abstract principles of ethics and ethical theory.

2. Intellectual Foundations

One of the particular challenges of teaching on the subject of professional and applied ethics involves integrating ideas and literature from one's particular profession and from the broader discipline of moral philosophy. We believe that instructors of social work ethics should rely specifically on three bodies of ideas and literature. First, instructors should draw on the literature that directly addresses the subject of social work ethics. As we noted earlier, this literature, unfortunately, is at present relatively sparse, though it is beginning to expand. Much of the literature that is currently available reviews the values and ethical principles that social workers are ordinarily expected to adhere to. Relatively few of the writings on social work ethics critically examine the philosophical issues that emerge in professional practice or discuss problems related to conflicts among values and ways of resolving them.

Second, instructors should draw on literature that introduces students to traditional schools of thought in moral philosophy concerning issues of normative ethics and metaethics. In particular, students should have some familiarity with the debates between the so-called *absolutists* and *relativists* concerning metaethical issues, and between the *deontologists* and *teleologists* (especially the utilitarians) concerning principles of normative ethics. Most courses on applied and professional ethics cannot afford to spend large amounts of time on the "classics" of moral philosophy (that is, the works of Plato, Aristotle, Kant, Bentham, Mill, Hume, Hobbes, among others), but students might at least be introduced to the names of these works, their authors, and their central ideas; it is important for practitioners to understand that contemporary ethical debates have their roots in ancient ideas and figures.[43] It is also useful for students to have some exposure to the ideas of more recent philosophers, such as G.E. Moore, John Dewey, and W.D. Ross, and contemporary philosophers, such as Kurt Baier, John Rawls, Robert Nozick, Alan Gewirth, William Frankena, J.J.C. Smart, and Bernard Williams.[44]

Finally, students should be introduced to the vast literature on the general subject of applied and professional ethics. In recent years there has been a burgeoning of articles, journals, monographs, and texts devoted entirely to the ethical dilemmas that members of professions such as law, medicine, business, nursing, journalism, engineering, and social work encounter in practice. This literature includes case studies, discussions of codes of ethics, attempts to apply abstract ethical principles to specific dilemmas, and theoretical discussions of specific issues such as truth-telling, the distribution of scarce resources, confidentiality, self-determination, whistle-blowing, and so forth.[45]

3. The Use of Case Material

As we observed earlier, the teaching of social work ethics should rely to a considerable degree on the examination of actual dilemmas that have arisen in practice. It is important to use cases in order to capture students' interest and in order to provide students with a taste of the kinds of dilemmas which they may encounter in their own careers.

We believe that a systematic review of ethical issues in social work should include an examination of the range of cases we outlined earlier, that is, cases related to (1) the delivery of services to individuals, families, and groups; (2) the design and implementation of social welfare policies and programs; and (3) relationships among professionals.[46] It is useful to draw on cases that have emerged from students' experiences and on cases that instructors have collected from their own experiences, the experiences of colleagues, films, and the literature. Reviewing students' cases can lend an air of relevance, realism, and salience which may not surround cases presented by the instructor. Discussion related to a case presented by a fellow student who is struggling to reconcile his or her beliefs about what is right and wrong can be unusually compelling, intense, and provocative. Such cases also present a particular challenge to the instructor who would need to—on the spot—attempt to relate the discussion of a student's case to the principles of ethics and ethical theories introduced elsewhere in the course. On the other hand, instructors who present cases from· their own collection have the benefit of being able to prepare an organized outline of the case and comments on the relationship between the facts in the case and principles of ethics. We suggest that instructors attempt to draw both on students' cases and cases from their own collections, being mindful of their respective advantages and disadvantages.

It is important that instructors examine cases in a systematic fashion in order to lend organization to class discussion and to present students with a model for assessing ethical dilemmas in practice. As a first step, instructors should present the facts of a case in the form of a vignette. Some instructors prefer to include considerable detail in order to reduce the amount of speculation engaged in and to focus discussion on a relatively narrow range of issues. Others prefer to provide only a broad outline of the facts in a case in order to encourage students to imagine and address a wide variety of hypothetical ethical dilemmas. Each approach has its strengths and weaknesses; both can be used effectively.

A related consideration regarding the presentation of cases concerns the "visibility" of the ethical dilemmas raised and suggested by the facts. Some cases will contain very visible ethical dilemmas, for example, those related to the right to life, the right to refuse treatment, confidentiality, and truth-telling. Other cases contain ethical dilemmas that are relatively subtle and camouflaged and need to have light shed on them in order to be detected. It is important for instructors to present students with both types of cases; we believe that it is important for social workers to develop skills that will enable them to scratch beneath the surface of cases in order to uncover ethical issues, in addition to skills for analyzing ethical dilemmas that are not so subtle. Students should also be presented with cases that are similar in some respects but sufficiently different to allow students to consider the relevance of such factors as age differences (and differences in other client characteristics), and differences in the nature of the social worker's specific responsibilities, the mission of the worker's employing organization, and legal requirements.

Once a case is presented, the instructor should help students identify the various ethical questions contained in it. Here the instructor should encourage students to consider (1) the various values at issue (for example, self-determination, promise-keeping, freedom of choice, truth-telling, equality, and need); (2) the relevant "actors" involved in the ethical dilemma, for example, the client, relatives, community residents, organizations, other professionals; and (3) important points in the decisionmaking process (that is, for example, whether certain considerations are especially important at the beginning stage or at the termination stage of a relationship with a client, or prior to the time when a particular policy is designed or implemented).

Finally, the instructor should organize discussion of the case around relevant principles of ethics and ethical theories. Students should be helped to see the similarities and differences between their arguments and the arguments presented by philosophers over the years. For example, questions should be raised about the relevance of a deontological or utilitarian approach to a given case, and about the strengths and weaknesses of these perspectives. Students should also be helped to realize when their arguments contain a logical inconsistency, or when they are inconsistent in their conclusions about the relative importance of competing values.[47] Students should also be encouraged to discuss the relevance of codes of ethics, religious beliefs, and cultural values in the analysis of ethical dilemmas.

The overall goal of case studies should be the identification and systematic discussion of ethical issues in social work. It is unrealistic to expect that the discussion of every case should end in a unanimous vote about what is right and wrong, or good and bad; this may occur only rarely. Rather, the principal aim of such discussions should be to have students critically (and tactfully) assess and challenge their own and one another's arguments. This does not mean that the instructor should endorse the relativistic view, or the view that since no absolute ethical standards are available, "anything goes." On the contrary, the instructor should encourage students to develop their convictions about what *is* right and wrong, and good and bad; and, as we concluded earlier, the instructor need not refrain from sharing his or her own opinions with the class.

4. Classroom Assignments

There are a number of assignments instructors can use effectively in the teaching of social work ethics. Written assignments can take several forms. First, term papers can be assigned in which students are expected to examine critically a particular case that contains substantial ethical questions and dilemmas, or a particular ethical issue that is relevant to the practice of social work. The student's analysis of a single case can follow the steps we outlined earlier regarding the analysis of cases in the classroom: (1) provide a brief outline of the scope of the paper, followed by a presentation of relevant facts and details; (2) identify the central ethical questions raised by the case and the relevant ethical concepts (considering the various values at issue, the relevant individuals and organizations, and important points in the decisionmaking process); and (3) present an organized discussion of the ethical questions raised by the case, drawing on ideas and literature in the areas of moral philosophy and theology, applied and professional ethics, and social work ethics. Students should be encouraged to formulate concrete opinions and to defend them, rather than to merely identify and describe issues. Such a case study should be viewed as a foreshadow of the kinds of ethical decisions and dilemmas students may face in the future; therefore, students should be expected to struggle with their own convictions and present thoughtful arguments in defense of their positions. Of course, it should not be expected that every student will conclude his or her study with a ringing unequivocal conclusion about the ethical questions raised by the case. Ethical dilemmas frequently resist being placed into neat and tidy packages from which no loose or hidden strings hang. Students who are inconclusive about specific issues should be expected, nonetheless, to present a detailed explanation of the various arguments the student finds persuasive and which seem to push him or her in more than one direction.

Papers that focus on a particular issue, rather than a specific case, can follow a similar format, with an introduction to the issue replacing the presentation of facts (step 1). There is a wide variety of controversial issues that students can examine, including issues such as the limits social workers should impose on clients' right to self-determination, abortion, and euthanasia (focusing on issues that are relevant to social workers), criteria for distributing limited federal social service funds, the phenomenon of whistle-blowing in social work, and ethical issues raised by the design of "workfare" programs. There is virtually no end to the list of important issues students can address. While many students will prefer to present their analyses in written form, instructors may want to invite a small number of students to present their case studies and issues to the class orally. (As a matter of principle, students should be encouraged to participate in oral discussions of ethical dilemmas. Being able to present arguments related to ethical dilemmas articulately and cogently is an important skill for social workers to cultivate.)

Instructors can also assign a variety of exercises to their students. In a course which has been taught at the University of Michigan, for example, students are expected to compile, as a first step, a "professional values biography," in which each student identifies his or her own personal values that have been brought to the course and factors that seem to have influenced the formulation of such values (for example, age, race, sex, marital and family status, ethnic or religious origins, the geographical area in which one was raised, historical events, and economic circumstances). The primary goal of this exercise is to help each student clarify and shape his or her own course goals and to help create a climate in which discussions of personal values can take place. Students in this course are required to prepare class exercises on value dilemmas drawn primarily from their personal experiences and concerns. The exercises are related to major social work values, such as self-determination, confidentiality, nondiscrimination, and so on. The students then are required to examine the criteria they would use (considering deontological values and utilitarian consequences) to determine a strategy for intervening in a particular case.[48] In a course that has been offered at the University of Tennessee (Nashville), students are assigned a variety of exercises, including (1) an analysis of changes in the content of NASW Codes of Ethics adopted or proposed between 1963 and the current 1980 Code; (2) an analysis of similarities and differences between the NASW Code of Ethics and codes of ethics of other professional organizations, such as the American Medical Association, American Bar Association, American Society of Public Administrators, and the National Association of Black Social Workers; (3) keeping a log of ethical dilemmas which arise during the course that are related to social work practice; (4) preparing a hypothetical staff development training course on the subject of professional (ethical) conduct; and (5) devising and critiquing a hypothetical plan for administrative monitoring of practitioners' conduct in a social service agency or organization.[49] In a course that is taught at the University of Missouri, films that depict ethical dilemmas related to social work are used successfully to help sharpen students' analytical skills.[50] Most courses that have been taught on the subject of social work ethics also rely to a considerable extent on actual cases for classroom exercises.

5. Integration of Class and Field Work

One of the enduring challenges in social work education is related to the integration of classroom instruction with students' experiences in their field placements. Instructors continually attempt to devise ways to relate the content of readings, lectures, and class discussions with the real-world events that predictably and unpredictably arise in field work. Throughout the history of social work education, such integration has been especially important to teachers of the so-called "methods" courses, that is, courses on casework, group work, family treatment, and community organization. Integration must also, however, be of concern to the teacher of social work ethics. It is important that students be helped to see that there are more than hypothetical connections between the discussions and analyses of ethical issues in the classroom and the genuine problems that arise in the actual practice of social work. In fact, one of the risks in organizing a course around philosophical ideas is that social work students— who, after all, tend to be more interested in *doing* than in ruminating qua philosopher—will grow impatient with excessive intellectual exercises and speculation that are hypothetical in nature. It is thus important for social workers to devise ways of consistently shuttling between the ideas, concerns, and principles of ethics on the one hand, and the workaday world of practitioners on the other.

Such integration can be attempted in several ways. First, in many schools, seminars, which have as their expressed purpose the integration of classroom material and field experiences, are held periodically. These field-work seminars can sometimes serve as a useful mechanism for discussing ethical issues. Unfortunately, however, these seminars are not necessarily (and probably only coincidentally, if ever) taught by a faculty member who is responsible for or genuinely interested in teaching on the subject of social work ethics. Of course, there is nothing to prevent the instructor of the field-work seminar from inviting a colleague who is knowledgeable in the area of social work ethics to occasionally participate in seminar sessions. Realistically, however, this form of integration, while at times useful, may prove difficult to achieve in many schools.

A second form of integration requires the cooperation of instructors of other nonethics courses. Under this arrangement, instructors of methods, policy, and research courses would be responsible for acknowledging and addressing in their courses ethical dilemmas that students encounter in the field. This approach has the advantage of helping students to realize that ethical dilemmas should be considered along with the learning of methods of intervention, theories of policy formulation and analysis, and methods of research. This too, however, can prove to be a difficult strategy to implement. Instructors of nonethics courses are frequently not interested in devoting a considerable amount of time to the examination of ethical issues; in addition, relatively few instructors of nonethics courses have the training or background that would enable them to address ethical issues in a rigorous, systematic fashion. This is a problem, but it is not insurmountable (we will have more to say about this in our discussion below of instructor qualifications and training). Once again, instructors of nonethics courses may invite a colleague who is concerned with ethical issues to participate in class sessions; however, our experience suggests that this is an approach not entirely dependable as a way to systematically integrate field experiences with class discussions of ethical issues.

Third, the field work supervisor can be encouraged to help students relate readings on the subject of social work ethics to ethical issues that arise in field placements. This, in fact, is one of the most preferred forms of integration; it is well known that students often count field-work supervisors among the most influential instructors and role models encountered during their educational careers. This form of integration can be especially useful if classroom faculty acquaint field-work supervisors with literature concerning social work ethics that can be referred to and drawn upon during the course of field-work supervision.

The instructor who is responsible for a discrete course on social work ethics is probably in the best position to integrate students' field experiences and class discussions of ethical issues. This instructor presumably is trained to relate principles of ethics to the analysis of concrete ethical dilemmas and presumably is interested in and committed to doing so. The obvious limitation of this strategy is that it stands to benefit only those students who enroll in a course on social work ethics.

As one would expect, then, these various approaches to integrating students' field experiences and class discussions of ethics have both advantages and disadvantages. The most important point we can make in this regard is that social work educators should place an emphasis on attempting to achieve this integration with whatever means are available, in order to enhance the relevance of classroom material related to principles of ethics and to encourage students to examine their field experiences, at least in part, through an ethical lens.

C. Placement in Curriculum

There are several important issues which need to be addressed regarding where and how instruction on social work ethics ought to be placed in the curriculum. The first issue is related to whether a separate course should be offered on the subject of social work ethics or whether this material ought to be sprinkled throughout the curriculum and included as portions of standard methods, policy, and research courses. We are quick to say that in an ideal world, students would be routinely exposed to ethical issues in the context of their nonethics courses and would also have the option of enrolling in a course devoted entirely to the subject of social work ethics. We know, however, that practical constraints which reside in many schools of social work (for example, with regard to scheduling, faculty resources, and course requirements) can affect the extent to which instruction related to social work ethics is introduced into the curriculum. We believe, nonetheless, that it is important for students—both undergraduate and graduate—to be exposed to the subject of social work ethics in their introductory courses on social work methods, social welfare policy, research, and human behavior. It is especially important that in the early days of their professional education students be encouraged to think about ethical issues and their relevance to decisions they will make in practice. Instructors of advanced nonethics courses should similarly strive to incorporate material on and discussions of ethics in their teaching.[51] We recognize that some instructors of nonethics courses may not feel adequately prepared to discuss ethical issues in a rigorous fashion; however, there are by now a sufficient number of introductory and provocative readings on the subject of applied ethics generally, and social work ethics in particular, so that instructors should not have difficulty mastering central ideas around which to organize lectures and discussions.[52] Guest speakers who are familiar and comfortable with the subject of applied and professional ethics can also be found in philosophy and theology departments of many colleges and universities.

In addition to attempting to introduce material on social work ethics in nonethics courses, we firmly believe that schools of social work should strive to develop an elective course on the subject for students who are especially interested in ethical issues in the profession. Such courses have been taught successfully in a number of schools of social work (though primarily to graduate students).

We are reluctant to advocate that each school offer a required course on social work ethics. This is so for at least two reasons. First, it is well known that students frequently are less enthusiastic about required courses than they are about electives. We have our doubts about the desirability of requiring students to enroll in a course on a subject that depends heavily on student participation, interest, and enthusiasm. Second, when a course is required of all students in a school, at least several instructors must be found to teach sections of the course (a course on social work ethics is especially ill-suited to a large lecture format); as we will discuss in greater detail below. However, most schools of social work would have considerable difficulty identifying several instructors who would be able, willing, and enthusiastic about teaching a course on social work ethics. We believe that it is essential that instructors of such a course be, at the very least, motivated to teach on the subject of social work ethics. We must do our best to avoid the problems that may arise when instructors of a course are required, subtly or otherwise, to teach on a subject about which they are neither well versed nor enthusiastic. The effect of students who are not excited about enrolling in a required course and an instructor who is less than skilled and excited about teaching the course combines in a chemistry which, *a fortiori*, should be avoided at all costs. We recognize, however, that some institutions (for example, schools of social work in sectarian colleges and universities) may have sound and well-publicized reasons for requiring a course on social work ethics. It should be noted, in fact, that several schools have required courses on social work ethics and have run them successfully.[53]

An issue which remains for us to consider is related specifically to schools that are in a position to offer a discrete course on social work ethics. At what point in the students' educational career should such a course be made available? We would argue that, in general, a discrete course on social work ethics should be offered to students some time between the midpoint and the end of their careers (for students in a two-year master's program this would, in most schools, entail the third and fourth semesters). There are several reasons for this assertion. First, we believe that during the first half of their educational careers, students should be primarily concerned with becoming acquainted with the contemporary boundaries, history, and methods of social work. As Pumphrey observed, the earliest months of professional education frequently function as a period of orientation in which students tend to be enthusiastic and eager to develop their professional bearings.[54] The orientation period is often followed by a period of critical questioning of social work's values and mission; this, in turn, is often followed by a final period of concern about one's career goals, competence, and ability to implement the profession's values.[55] We believe that it may be best to offer a course on social work ethics to students after they have had an opportunity to wet their professional feet and are at a point in their education where they are inclined to assess critically the values and mission of the profession and have had a chance to begin to formulate their career goals. This is not to suggest that students should not be exposed to ethical issues during the early part of their education; on the contrary, it is very important to broach these issues in the context of introductory nonethics courses. Rather, we believe that, given a choice, a discrete course on social work ethics is best offered to students who have had an opportunity to develop a solid understanding of the profession of social work and are close to making commitments about their own professional priorities and activities.[56]

D. Instructor Qualifications and Training

Among the most pressing issues related to the teaching of social work ethics is the subject of instructor qualifications and training. In the relatively recent history of applied and professional ethics, there has been considerable debate about the credentials and training that instructors should have. An extreme point of view is that extensive training in moral philosophy and ethical theory should be a prerequisite for teaching on the subject. A more moderate position is that instructors should have at least some familiarity with central ideas and literature from the field of moral philosophy, but that it is more important for instructors to be thoroughly familiar with the practice of the relevant profession than for them to be well versed and steeped in moral philosophy and ethical theory. Our own position is that the instructor of a course on social work ethics should, first of all, be a member of the profession and thoroughly familiar with its history, traditions, and methods. The ideal instructor will also have had the opportunity for some formal training in moral philosophy and ethical theory, such that he or she is both knowledgeable about and comfortable with presenting the various ethical arguments, schools of thought, and lines of reasoning that have developed over the years. As we observed above, we firmly believe that instruction on social work ethics should depend on and integrate ideas and materials from the discipline of ethics and the field of social work. We recognize that there are relatively few social work educators who have had the opportunity to obtain formal training in ethics.[57] We believe, however, that prospective and current social work educators who are interested in ethical issues in the profession should do their best to obtain such training. Although course work in moral philosophy and ethics would be the most desirable form of training, social work educators who have the temperament for studying philosophical literature can absorb a great deal from the vast writings (introductory and advanced) on the subjects of ethical theory and professional and applied ethics.

Social work educators who are responsible for courses on ethics can also collaborate with moral philosophers and theologians interested in ethical issues. Such collaboration can take several forms. First, philosophers and theologians can be consulted about theories, concepts, themes, issues, and literature which might be included in a course on social work ethics. Second, philosophers and theologians can be invited to deliver guest lectures which would illustrate ways of applying philosophical ideas to ethical problems in social work. Finally, in some settings it may be desirable to invite a philosopher or theologian to coteach a course on social work ethics along with members of the social work faculty. Such an approach can have the advantage of providing students with instruction from faculty who have a command of material related both to social work and moral philosophy. We must caution, however, that team-teaching is not always a desirable or effective alternative. It can be an expensive way to teach, and in an era of strained and diminished educational resources, administrators of schools of social work and departments of philosophy may be reluctant to allocate their faculty in such a manner. In addition, courses which are team-taught sometimes suffer some lack of coordination, consistency, and organization. It is important that efforts to team-teach a course on social work ethics be designed carefully and that deliberate attempts be made to select instructors whose teaching styles, goals and substantive materials are complementary. It is also important for collaborators to pay close attention to the division of intellectual labor, that is, the extent to which the social work educator will concentrate on social work-related material and the philosopher or theologian on the philosophical material, the extent to which the collaborators will present students with a unified point of view, and the extent to which the collaborators will encourage debate between themselves. A well-planned team-taught course can be a valuable learning experience for students and a practical teaching strategy for social work educators who do not feel sufficiently comfortable with or trained to present philosophical material on ethics.

IV. Conclusion

The profession of social work has come a long way since its emergence in the nineteenth century. The mission and methods of the profession have changed substantially since the days of the charity organization societies, friendly visitors, and settlement houses. Along with changes in our purposes and strategies have also come important changes in social work education. Training programs, which were once organized primarily around transmitting the art of casework, now include substantial components on the subjects of social welfare policy, community organization, management and administration, group work, and methods of research, in addition to training in an expanded range of clinical techniques.

Although the bulk of social work education is devoted to mastering methods of intervention and evaluation—and appropriately so—in recent years many educators have come to realize that the practice of social work is often burdened with difficult ethical questions and dilemmas. It is now clear that most social workers will encounter ethical problems throughout their careers which an understanding of methods of intervention and research alone will not help them resolve. Many of us are now aware that puzzling and demanding questions of right and wrong, good and bad, and duty and obligation call for reflection on and discussion of ethical concepts, and that social work education needs to do its part to ensure that practitioners are sensitive to the ethical aspects of professional work and have skills that will enable them to identify and assess ethical issues and dilemmas.

The emerging interest in social work ethics is part of a general heightening of interest in professional and applied ethics. There is ample evidence to indicate that members of professions such as law, business, medicine, journalism, nursing, engineering, psychology, and social work are paying more and more attention to the ethical dimensions of their work and are incorporating ethical content into their training programs, writings, and conferences with greater regularity. We believe that this is a healthy development for the professions; we also believe that it is important for educators to do what they can to help sustain the momentum that now exists and to help avoid having the subject of professional ethics regarded as merely a fashionable and ephemeral twist in academic pursuits. In order to do so, it will be important for educators to be mindful of several issues related to teaching professional ethics.

A. The Persistence of Ethical Dilemmas

Those who are somewhat skeptical about discussions of professional ethics sometimes claim that, given the recalcitrance of many ethical dilemmas and the frequent inability of professionals to agree on ways of resolving them, extended debate about ethical issues is nearly (if not entirely) pointless. Ethical dilemmas are, they assert, matters about which one can only conjecture and speculate, and that these dilemmas stubbornly resist solution.

It is true that many ethical dilemmas encountered by professionals are disconcertingly complex and are subject to a wide variety of opinions. It is also true that many of the most important ethical dilemmas that professionals face are ones that professionals may forever debate. We do not believe, however, that these enduring features of ethical dilemmas must lead us to conclude that reflection on and discussion of them is not worthwhile. On the contrary, we would argue just the opposite. It is the compelling nature of many ethical dilemmas that leads, in the first place, to widely divergent and strongly held opinions. Differences of opinion about trivial matters are undeserving of substantial attention. But long-standing debates about important matters of ethics—important because of the significance of the consequences involved for the well-being of people—indicate something about what we value most as professionals and serve as a barometer of changing professional concerns.

Many of the most important ethical debates will not be settled easily, if at all; we firmly believe, however, that there is something of value in encouraging professionals to distinguish between the ethical and nonethical dimensions of their work, to think carefully about the ethical implications of their own decisions and actions, and to engage in constructive dialogue with colleagues about ethical issues. The teaching of professional ethics will not necessarily produce practitioners who are more moral, that we know;[58] they can, however, help practitioners to become more self-conscious about the ethical aspects of their professional activities. As Derek Bok has observed:

> . . . Even if courses in applied ethics turned out to have no effect whatsoever on the moral development of our students, they would still make a contribution. There is value to be gained from any course that forces students to think carefully and rigorously about complex human problems. . . . Although the point is still unproved, it does seem plausible to suppose that the students in these courses will become more alert in perceiving ethical issues, more aware of the reasons underlying moral principles, and more equipped to reason carefully in applying these principles to concrete cases. Will they behave more ethically? We may never know. But surely the experiment is worth trying, for the goal has never been more important to the quality of the society in which we live.[59]

B. The Importance of Ethical Analysis

One of the concerns we have voiced repeatedly is the tendency in social work to expose students to traditional social work values (for example, self-determination, individual dignity, confidentiality, freedom) and to the profession's Code of Ethics without *critically* examining the origins and content of these values. Though it is not unusual for the general subject of values and ethics to be broached in classes, it is rare that instructors devote a substantial amount of time to a rigorous and systematic analysis of ethical issues in the profession. The remedy, we believe, is two-sided. First, social work educators must avoid giving students the impression that traditional social work values and ethical prescriptions have prima facie validity that does not require critical analysis or is not subject to metaethical questions about the meaning of ethical terms or the justification of ethical guidelines. Second, educators must focus on the application of principles of ethics to the analysis of the kinds of ethical dilemmas that social workers tend to encounter in practice. They must focus in particular on the difficult choices social workers must frequently make among competing values, and the reasons that might be given for concluding that one value should take precedence over another. Thus, the thrust of teaching should be on *ethical analysis*, rather than only on a review of traditional social work values and the profession's Code of Ethics.

C. The Future of Ethics in Social Work Education

There is reason to believe that the subject of professional ethics will continue to attract substantial attention in future years. It appears that the growth of interest in ethical issues represents far more than an intellectual fad which is merely riding the crest of a prominent wave. We are at a special place in history that has given rise to widespread concern about ethical matters. We know, on the one hand, that we are enjoying the fruits of technological advances that our ancestors could hardly have imagined possible. In many respects, the lives of those who live in modern industrial communities are less encumbered than the lives of any of our forebears. But we also know very well that the advances that have smoothed out many of life's bumps and perils have been accompanied by stiff prices. In important ways, we have replaced our fears of nature's forces with fears of the uses to which the mechanisms which we have invented for controlling or affecting life's natural forces might be put. We thus have contemporary concerns about euthanasia, prompted in part by medical advances that can sustain lives *ad infinitum*, and concerns about nuclear hazards, prompted in part by scientific advances that were intended to expand sources of energy. In addition, we are faced with perplexing issues and difficult decisions related to the role of government in welfare matters, the social and economic roots of poverty, and the allocation of limited resources. It is evident that the special unprecedented knowledge and problems peculiar to this day and age force us to entertain difficult questions of ethics that could not have been of concern to our predecessors.

An important by-product of the variety of technological advances we have witnessed in recent years (especially within the past century) and contemporary social maladies has been the emergence of professions organized around either the technology itself (for example, engineering) or around the activities of individuals who respond to the complexity and the social problems that have trailed our technological advances (for example, lawyers, psychologists, and social workers). The growth of interest in professional ethics is no accident. The professions are themselves coming of age and are beginning to recognize more than ever before that their work produces or brings them face to face with difficult ethical dilemmas. Many training programs are now attempting to convey to students that attention to questions of ethics must accompany the learning of technical skills.

This is certainly true of the profession of social work, though we have come to this realization somewhat later than many other professions. It is clear that in the future practitioners will be faced with difficult decisions about the extent of their duty to aid those in need, the role of government in welfare matters, and the distribution of scarce or limited resources. Social workers will encounter hard ethical choices in their work with individuals, families, and groups, in the design and implementation of social welfare policies and programs, and in their relationships with professional colleagues. It is important for social work educators to assume major responsibility for introducing prospective practitioners to ethical issues in the profession and to help students develop skills that will enable them to assess ethical dilemmas carefully. As Muriel Pumphrey observed in her 1959 study of the teaching of values and ethics in social work education: "It seems axiomatic that if social work is a heavily value-laden profession, its values also must be communicated to new recruits, and understood and accepted by them in their efforts to develop into *bona fide* professional representatives."[60]

D. The Efficacy of Ethics

Students enrolled in courses on professional ethics sometimes ask, "Can ethics really make a difference?" This is a difficult question to answer. We know, for example, that impassioned statements about right and wrong, and moral duty and obligation, do not necessarily carry much weight with individuals who make important decisions about social welfare. Legislators and bureaucrats will not necessarily be persuaded by thoughtful arguments about the concepts of justice, truth, equality, and so forth. Political bargaining and economic incentives will, in many cases, shape social welfare policy more than any theory of ethics possibly could. The self-interested motives or personality traits of individual social workers can also have a greater effect on the actions taken regarding a particular client than careful rumination about principles of ethics. We should not be naive about the force of ethics in the daily deliberations of many social workers.

What, then, can we expect from ethics? First, if we do our job as social work educators well, we can expect that individual students will walk away from our courses and discussions with a greater appreciation of the fact that professional decisions are not always of a technical nature and frequently require consideration of ethical issues. Such an awareness can help social workers realize that in addition to asking the question, "What works?" one should often ask, "Is it right?" There clearly are important differences between these queries; the extent to which they are addressed and the answers practitioners provide to them can have profound consequences for the quality of the lives of individuals.

Exposing students to the subject of social work ethics can also move our profession much closer to the ideals we have embraced—with good reason—for nearly a century. Concepts such as justice, equality of opportunity, and self-determination are not trivial. If these values strike us as platitudinous, it is because there is something compelling about them that leads us to cite them frequently. There is no guarantee that critical discussion of such ideals will enable us to quickly fulfill them, but it is not unrealistic to think that the more we think about them the greater is the probability that we will at least *move toward* fulfilling them. We are much less willing these days to conclude that one value is as good as another; relativism is on the decline, and exposing social workers to the merits of various principles of ethics and to ethical dilemmas in the profession can do much to help practitioners separate what we are willing to tolerate in our world from what we find unconscionable and, as a consequence, strive to change.

It is true that debates about ethics will not necessarily change anything; the decisions and actions of individuals, committees, agencies, and governments are frequently the product of determinants that are either out of our control or just barely within our grasp. Yet, each of us must at times make significant personal choices among competing options and decisions about whether certain courses of action, which can dramatically affect the lives of others, are worth pursuing. The private answers we provide ourselves in such instances *can* make a difference. It is important for social work educators to help ensure that prospective members of the profession are aware of their responsibility to consider the ethical aspects of these decisions and the effects they can have on the clients who, after all, are our principal concern.

Notes

1. Robert Treat Paine, Jr., "The Work of Volunteer Visitors of the Associated Charities Among the Poor," *Journal of Social Science* 12 (1880):113.

2. Alexander Johnson, *Adventures in Social Welfare: Being Reminiscences of Things, Thoughts and Folks During Forty Years of Social Work* (Fort Wayne, Indiana: Fort Wayne Printing Company, 1923).

3. Roy Lubove, *The Professional Altruist: The Emergence of Social Work as a Career, 1880–1930* (New York: Atheneum, 1975), p. 83.

4. Muriel W. Pumphrey, *The Teaching of Values and Ethics in Social Work Education* (New York: Council on Social Work Education, 1959).

5. See Arlien Johnson, "Educating Professional Social Workers for Ethical Practice," *Social Service Review* 29 (1955):125–36.

6. *The Teaching of Ethics in Higher Education* (Hastings-on-Hudson, New York: The Hastings Center, 1980).

7. Ibid., p. 20

8. Ibid., p. 21.

9. Frederick Suppe, "The Search for Philosophic Understanding of Scientific Studies," in *The Structure of Scientific Theories*, ed. Frederick Suppe (Urbana, Ill.: University of Illinois Press, 1974), p. 283.

10. For example, see the Bibliography in *The Teaching of Ethics in Higher Education*, pp. 91–103

11. Martha Brunswick Heineman, "The Obsolete Scientific Imperative in Social Work Research," *Social Service Review*, 55 (1981) 371–97.

12. See Roy Lubove, *The Professional Altruist*; Walter I. Trattner, *From Poor Law to Welfare State* (New York: Free Press, 1974); and Kathleen Woodroofe, *From Charity to Social Work in England and the United States* (Toronto: University of Toronto Press, 1962).

13. See *Encyclopedia of Social Work*, 17th ed., (1977), s.v. "Abraham Flexner."

14. See "Letter of Transmittal" to membership of the Council on Social Work Education from the Commission on Educational Planning, March 8, 1981.

15. In 1955, Arlien Johnson reported that 15 of 27 member schools of the Council on Social Work Education, which had enrollments of 60 or more full-time students, taught ethics in a special course. (see Arlien Johnson, "Educating Professional Social Workers for Ethical Practice"). Our unscientific, but informed, impression is that the percentage of schools that now offer a discrete course on the subject has declined substantially.

16. See Roland G. Meinert, "Values in Social Work Called Dysfunctional Myth," *Journal of Social Welfare* 6 (1980):11. Meinert reports that a content analysis of more than 2,500 course descriptions from bulletins of schools of social work for the year 1975 revealed only 19 course descriptions (less than 1 percent) that contained the words values, ethics, morals, beliefs, or philosophy in them.

17. See Suanna J. Wilson, *Confidentiality in Social Work*. (New York: Free Press, 1978).

18. See Immanuel Kant, "On a Supposed Right to Lie from Benevolent Motives," in *The Critique of Practical Reason and Other Writings in Moral Philosophy*, ed. and trans. Lewis White Beck (Chicago: University of Chicago Press, 1949), pp. 346–50.

19. See Sissela Bok, *Lying: Moral Choice in Public and Private Life* (New York: Vintage Books, 1979).

20. See Gerald Dworkin, "Paternalism," in *Morality and the Law*, ed. Richard A. Wasserstrom (Belmont, California: Wadsworth, 1971), pp. 107–26; and Joel Feinberg, "Legal Paternalism," in *Today's Moral Problems*, ed. Richard Wasserstrom (New York: Macmillan, 1975), pp. 33–49.

21. See also the various articles on self-determination contained in F.E. McDermott, ed., *Self-Determination in Social Work* (London: Routledge and Kegan Paul, 1975).

22. See Sir Isaiah Berlin, *Four Essays on Liberty* (London: Oxford University Press, 1969), pp. 121–34. Negative liberty is contrasted with "positive" liberty, or the freedom to be one's own master and to make choices.

23. See, for example, Richard Wasserstrom, "The Obligation to Obey the Law," in *Today's Moral Problems*, ed. Richard Wasserstrom, pp. 358–84.

24. See J. J. C. Smart and Bernard Williams, *Utilitarianism: For and Against* (Cambridge: Cambridge University Press, 1973), p. 10.

25. See William K. Frankena, *Ethics*, 2nd ed. (Englewood Cliffs, N.J.: Prentice-Hall, 1973), pp. 48–52.

26. See Robert Pinker, *The Idea of Welfare* (London: Heinemann, 1979), pp. 75–94.

27. Sissela Bok, "Whistleblowing and Professional Responsibility," *New York University Education Quarterly* 11 (1980):2.

28. See ibid. and Helen Dudar, "The Price of Blowing the Whistle," *New York Times Magazine*, October 30, 1979, pp. 41–54; Ralph Nader, Peter Petkas, and Kate Blackwell, *Whistle Blowing* (New York: Grossman, 1972); Charles Peter and Taylor Branch, *Blowing the Whistle* (New York: Praeger, 1972).

29. See Sissela Bok, *Lying: Moral Choice in Public and Private Life*.

30. See Suanna J. Wilson, *Confidentiality in Social Work*.

31. See Mildred Mailick and Ardythe Ashley, "Interprofessional Collaboration: Challenge to Advocacy," *Social Casework* 62 (1981):131–37.

32. See *Encyclopedia Britannica*, 15th ed., (1978), s.v. "Ethics"; William K. Frankena, *Ethics*; Walter Stace, "Ethical Absolutism and Ethical Relativism," in *Ethics in Perspective*, eds. Karsten J. Struhl and Paula Rothenberg Struhl (New York: Random House, 1975), pp. 51–60.

33. See Muriel W. Pumphrey, *The Teaching of Values and Ethics in Social Work Education*, especially pp. 141–43.

34. See *Encyclopedia Britannica*, s.v. "Ethics"; William K. Frankena, *Ethics*.

35. Ibid.

36. See William K. Frankena, *Ethics*, pp. 34–43; J. J. C. Smart and Bernard Williams, *Utilitarianism: For and Against*; Samuel Gorovitz, ed., *Utilitarianism* (Indianapolis: Bobbs-Merrill, 1971); Frederic G. Reamer, "Ethical Content in Social Work," *Social Casework* 61 (1980):531–40.

37. See John Rawls, *A Theory of Justice* (Cambridge, Mass.: Harvard University Press, 1971), pp. 42–45.

38. See Arlien Johnson, "Educating Professional Social Workers for Ethical Practice"; Muriel W. Pumphrey, *The Teaching of Values and Ethics in Social Work Education*.

39. *The Teaching of Ethics in Higher Education*, p. 48.

40. Ibid., p. 61.

41. Muriel W. Pumphrey, *The Teaching of Values and Ethics in Social Work Education*, p. 29.

42. See Chapter II for an outline and review of issues and dilemmas related to normative ethics and metaethics around which a course can be organized.

43. It is probably safe to assume that most social work students will not have had a thorough introduction to or grounding in moral philosophy. Philosophical

readings used in a course on social work ethics should probably be of an introductory nature (see Bibliography). Some instructors will also want to expose students to introductory readings on theological ethics.

44. See Bibliography.

45. Ibid. Instructors may also find it useful to incorporate readings from history and fiction to illustrate and illuminate ethical issues.

46. See Chapter II.

47. It may be useful for instructors to introduce students to basic principles of inductive and deductive logic and to common logical fallacies. We have found two references particularly useful for this purpose: Dwight J. Ingle, *Is It Really So? A Guide to Clear Thinking* (Philadelphia: Westminster Press, 1976); Wesley C. Salmon, *Logic* (Englewood Cliffs, N.J.: Prentice-Hall, 1963).

48. This course has been taught by Sydney E. Bernard of the School of Social Work, University of Michigan.

49. This course has been taught by Mary H. Bloch of the School of Social Work, University of Tennessee (Nashville).

50. This course has been taught by Frederic G. Reamer. Useful films can be obtained from the Joseph P. Kennedy, Jr., Foundation, Film Services, 999 Asylum Avenue, Hartford, Connecticut 06105.

51. For a review of issues that can be raised in nonethics courses and that are related to various approaches or methods of practice, see Muriel W. Pumphrey, *The Teaching of Values and Ethics in Social Work Education, pp. 50–61.*

52. See Chapter II and Bibliography.

53. For example, at the National Catholic School of Social Service, Catholic University of America, and the School of Social Service, St. Louis University.

54. Muriel W. Pumphrey, *The Teaching of Values and Ethics in Social Work Education*, pp. 65–74.

55. Ibid.

56. We recognize that instructors of many nonethics courses use similar reasoning to argue that their courses should be offered during the middle or end of students' programs. We have thus stated what we believe to be preferable *in principle*, knowing that a course on social work ethics may need to "compete" with nonethics courses for room in the second half of a school's curriculum.

57. This is a problem that apparently plagues all of the professions. See *The Teaching of Ethics in Higher Education*, pp. 62–66.

58. As Arjay Miller, former Dean of the Stanford Business School, observed, "I believe we ought to be doing more, but I'm not sure exactly what. . . . It's a problem of motivation and basic human values. There are a lot

of people in jail today who have passed ethics courses." (Cited in *The Teaching of Ethics in Higher Education*, p. 6.)

59. Derek Bok, "Can Ethics be Taught?" *Change* 8 (1976):30.

60. Muriel W. Pumphrey, *The Teaching of Values and Ethics in Social Work Education*, p. 12.

Bibliography

I. Books and Articles on Teaching Applied and Professional Ethics

Bok, Derek. "Can Ethics Be Taught?" *Change* 8 (1976):26–30.

Bok, Sissela, and Callahan, Daniel. "Teaching Applied Ethics." *Radcliffe Quarterly* 69 (1979):30–33.

Callahan, Daniel, and Bok, Sissela. "The Role of Applied Ethics in Learning." *Change* 11 (1979):23–27.

———, eds. *Ethics Teaching in Higher Education*. New York: Plenum Press, 1980.

Montefiore, Alan. "Moral Philosophy and the Teaching of Morality." *Harvard Educational Review* 35 (1965):435–49.

Ozar, David. "Teaching Philosophy and Teaching Values." *Teaching Philosophy* 2 (1979):1–10.

The Teaching of Ethics in Higher Education. Hastings-on-Hudson, N.Y. The Hastings Center, 1980.

Walzer, Michael. "Teaching Morality." *The New Republic*, June 10, 1978:12–14.

II. Moral Philosophy

Baier, Kurt. *The Moral Point of View*. New York: Random House, 1965.

Berlin, Isaiah. *Four Essays on Liberty*. Oxford: Oxford University Press, 1968.

Bok, Sissela. *Lying: Moral Choice in Public and Private Life*. New York: Pantheon, 1978.

Brandt, Richard B. *Ethical Theory*. Englewood Cliffs, N.J.: Prentice-Hall, 1959.

Diener, Edward, and Crandall, Rick. *Ethics in Social and Behavioral Research*. Chicago: University of Chicago Press, 1978.

Donagan, Alan. *The Theory of Morality*. Chicago: University of Chicago Press, 1977.

Frankena, William K. *Ethics*. 2nd ed. Englewood Cliffs, N.J.: Prentice-Hall, 1973.

Fried, Charles. *Right and Wrong*. Cambridge, Mass.: Harvard University Press, 1978.

Gewirth, Alan. *Reason and Morality*. Chicago: University of Chicago Press, 1978.

Hancock, Roger N. *Twentieth Century Ethics*. New York: Columbia University Press, 1974.

MacIntyre, Alasdair. *A Short History of Ethics*. New York: Macmillan, 1966.

Nozick, Robert, *Anarchy, State, and Utopia*. New York: Basic Books, 1974.

Rawls, John. *A Theory of Justice*. Cambridge, Mass.: Harvard University Press, 1971.

Ross, W.D. *The Right and the Good*. Oxford: Clarendon Press, 1930.

Sellars, W. S., and Hospers, John, eds. *Readings in Ethical Theory*. 2nd ed. New York: Appleton-Century-Crofts, 1970.

Smart, J. J. C. and Williams, Bernard. *Utilitarianism: For and Against*. Cambridge: Cambridge University Press, 1973.

Wasserstrom, Richard, ed. *Today's Moral Problems*. 2nd ed. New York: Macmillan, 1979.

Williams, Bernard. *Morality: An Introduction to Ethics*. New York: Harper & Row, 1972.

III. Social Work Ethics

Abramson, Marcia. "Ethical Dilemmas for Social Workers in Discharge Planning." *Social Work in Health Care*, forthcoming.

Code of Ethics. New York: National Association of Social Workers, 1980.

Emmet, Dorothy. "Ethics and the Social Worker." *British Journal of Psychiatric Social Work* 6 (1962):165–72.

Encyclopedia of Social Work, 17th ed. s.v. "Ethics in Social Work," by Alan Keith-Lucas.

Frankel, Charles. "Social Philosophy and the Professional Education of Social Workers." *Social Service Review* 33 (1959):345–59.

Levy, Charles S. "The Context of Social Work Ethics." *Social Work* 17 (1972):95–101.

———. "The Value Base of Social Work." *Journal of Education for Social Work* 9 (1973):34–42.

———. *Social Work Ethics*. New York: Human Sciences Press, 1976.

Lewis, Harold. "Morality and the Politics of Practice." *Social Casework* 53 (1972):404–17.

McDermott, F. E., ed. *Self-Determination in Social Work*. London: Routledge and Kegan Paul, 1975.

Plant, Raymond. *Social and Moral Theory in Casework*. London: Routledge and Kegan Paul, 1970.

Pumphrey, Muriel W. *The Teaching of Values and Ethics in Social Work Education*. New York: Council on Social Work Education, 1959.

Reamer, Frederic G. *Ethical Dilemmas in Social Service*. New York: Columbia University Press, in press.

———. "Ethical Dilemmas in the Practice of Social Work." *Social Work*, in press.

———. "Ethical Content in Social Work." *Social Casework* 61 (1980):531–40.

———. "Fundamental Ethical Issues in Social Work: An Essay Review." *Social Service Review* 53 (1979):229–43.

Timms, Noel, and Watson, David, eds. *Philosophy in Social Work*. London: Routledge and Kegan Paul, 1978.

Vigilante, Joseph L. "Between Values and Science: Education for the Profession During a Moral Crisis *or* is Proof Truth?" *Journal of Education for Social Work* 10 (1974):107–15.

Wilson, Suanna J. *Confidentiality in Social Work*. New York: Free Press, 1978.